CW00919697

The Microsoft Word Handbook 2023

An ultimate Reference Guide to Mastering word Features and improving productivity

For permissions requests, write to the publisher at the address below:

Micheal Ambrose

ambrosemicheal459@gmail.com

Cover design by Micheal Ambrose

Library of Congress Cataloging-in-Publication Data

Ambrose, Micheal

The Microsoft Word Handbook 2023: An ultimate Reference Guide to Mastering word Features and improving productivity

ISBN: 9798398294774

Printed in 2023

First Edition: 2023

Dedication

This book is dedicated to my loving family, who has supported and encouraged me every step of the way. Your unwavering love and belief in me have been my guiding light.

To my friends, for their constant inspiration and companionship throughout this journey. Your presence has brought joy and warmth to my life.

To my mentors, whose wisdom and guidance have shaped my perspective and fueled my ambition. Your knowledge and encouragement have been invaluable.

To all the readers, who embark on this literary adventure. May this book captivate your imagination, expand your horizons, and ignite your passion for learning.

Lastly, to the countless individuals who strive to make this world a better place. May this book serve as a reminder of our collective potential and the importance of pursuing our dreams with unwavering determination.

Thank you all for being a part of this incredible journey. Your unwavering support and belief in me have made this book possible.

With deepest gratitude,

MIcheal Ambrose

Table of Contents

Who this Book is For

1. Everyday Users of MS Word: If you use Microsoft Word for your daily work or personal tasks, this book serves as a valuable reference guide. It will help you navigate through the features and functionalities of MS Word, enhancing your productivity and efficiency in creating and formatting documents.

2. Learners of MS Word: If you are new to Microsoft Word or seeking to enhance your skills, this book is an excellent resource. It provides step-by-step guides to help you grasp the fundamentals and master advanced techniques. Whether you are a beginner or intermediate user, this book will support your learning journey.

3. Students in School: Students can benefit greatly from this book as it covers essential aspects of MS Word commonly used in academic settings. From formatting essays and reports to creating tables, this book provides clear instructions and techniques that can streamline your document creation process and improve your academic work.

4. Professionals and Business Users: Professionals in various fields, such as business, administration, or research, can leverage the knowledge in this book to optimize their use of MS Word. From creating professional documents with consistent formatting to utilizing advanced features for data organization and collaboration, this book caters to the needs of professionals looking to maximize their productivity.

5. Individuals Seeking to Enhance Productivity: Whether you are an entrepreneur, writer, or anyone who relies on MS Word for productivity, this book provides valuable insights and time-saving techniques. You will learn how to customize settings, leverage automation tools, and adopt best practices that can significantly boost your efficiency when working with MS Word.

6. Anyone Interested in MS Word: Ultimately, this book is for anyone with an interest in Microsoft Word. Whether you want to improve your document creation skills, explore advanced features, or simply gain a better understanding of this widely used word processing software, this book caters to your curiosity and equips you with practical knowledge.

Introduction

In today's fast-paced world, effective utilization of technology is paramount to success. From students working on assignments to business professionals creating reports and writers crafting their next masterpieces, Microsoft Word has become an indispensable tool for individuals and professionals alike.

The Microsoft Word Handbook 2023 is a definitive resource designed to empower users to unleash the full potential of Microsoft Word. This book serves as a comprehensive reference guide, providing step-by-step instructions, practical tips, and valuable insights to help you navigate and utilize the vast array of features and tools available in Microsoft Word.

The journey begins with an exploration of the basic features of Microsoft Word. You will learn how to create and save documents, format text to enhance readability and visual appeal, and leverage various tools to streamline your workflow. Building upon this foundation, we delve into advanced formatting techniques, including working with shapes, images, and tables. You will discover how to manipulate document layouts, create professional templates, and utilize styles to maintain consistency throughout your documents.

As we progress, we uncover the hidden features of Microsoft Word that are often overlooked but can significantly enhance your productivity. From optimizing document organization and utilizing efficient page layouts to leveraging the power of headers, footers, and margins, you will gain insights into leveraging the full potential of Microsoft Word's advanced capabilities.

Collaboration and document sharing are vital aspects of modern document management, and this book provides comprehensive coverage on these topics. You will learn how to co-author documents in real-time, incorporate comments and track changes, and protect your documents from unauthorized access. Additionally, we delve into the process of merging data using mail merge, creating table of contents for efficient navigation, and automating tasks with macros to save valuable time.

Throughout the book, we provide tips and strategies to boost your productivity in Microsoft Word. You will discover add-ins and additional resources that can extend the functionality of Microsoft Word, allowing you to tailor the software to your specific needs and work more efficiently.

Whether you are a student, a professional, or an enthusiast, The Microsoft Word Handbook 2023 equips you with the knowledge and skills necessary to become proficient in this powerful word processing software. With its user-friendly approach, this guide will empower you to create polished documents, streamline your workflow, collaborate effectively, and unlock the full potential of Microsoft Word. Get ready to embark on a transformative journey as you master the art of productivity with Microsoft Word.

Journey into Microsoft Word

Microsoft word is a Word processing application used to create, edit, format, and manipulate text-based documents. It provides a comprehensive set of tools and features that aid in document creation and formatting, making it an essential tool for individuals, businesses, and organizations worldwide.

In this book we will explore amazing features of Microsoft Word and guide you step by step on how to use them. This book is designed to get straight to the point without any long stories or distractions. Our goal is to make this book serve as a reference and to help you understand and make the most of Microsoft Word in a simple and straightforward way. Get ready to embark on a journey of discovery as we learn about the essence of Microsoft Word and how it can be a valuable tool for you.

In this chapter, we'll look at Microsoft Word's fundamental features and how to make the best use of them. We'll begin by introducing the Word user interface and getting acquainted with its many components. After that, we'll discuss Word's fundamental features, including how to create, format, and edit text, add photos and graphics, and use templates to speed up your work process.

You'll have a firm grasp of Microsoft Word's fundamental capabilities by the end of this chapter and be prepared to use it to produce documents with a professional appearance. This chapter will offer helpful tips on how to utilize Word to its full potential whether you're a novice or a seasoned user.

The Microsoft Word Interface

The interface of Word is intuitive and consists of various components that are organized in a logical and user-friendly manner. These elements include the Ribbon, Quick Access Toolbar, Document Area,

Status Bar, Scroll Bar, and Insertion Point. Each of these elements plays a vital role in helping users navigate and utilize the software efficiently. By understanding the interface of Microsoft Word, users can take full advantage of the program's features and create professional-looking documents with ease.

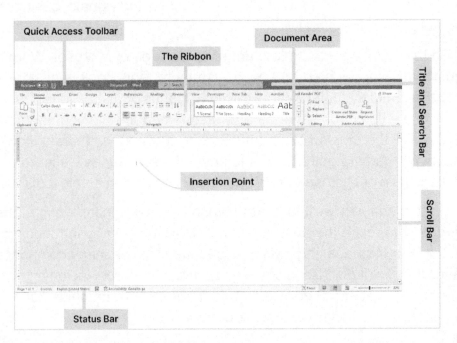

Ribbon: The Ribbon is a graphical user interface that shows several tabs with different groupings of actions listed under each one. The commands are arranged logically into categories and gathered behind tabs. To make it simple to locate the commands and finish a task fast, the Ribbon was created.

Quick Access Toolbar: This toolbar can be positioned above or below the Ribbon and is fully customizable. Save, Undo, and Redo are among the frequently used commands that may be accessed with just one click.

Document Area: You create and update documents in the Document Area. You can add text, pictures, tables, charts, and other components to the blank canvas.

Status Bar: The status bar, which is at the bottom of the screen, displays details about the open document, including its page count, word count, and zoom level.

Scroll Bar: The Scroll Bar is used to navigate through a document. It allows you to move up and down, left and right, and zoom in and out of the document.

Insertion Point: The blinking cursor that denotes where the next character will be entered into in the document is called the Insertion Point.

Templates: Templates are pre-designed papers that serve as a jumping off point for writing a certain type of document, like a résumé, letter, or brochure. There are numerous pre-built templates available in Word, and you can also create your own.

Microsoft word consist of numerous features from everyday use features for typing and editing documents to features used for collaborating, automating which in general increase the productivity of a Microsoft word user.

Throughout this book we would focus our attention on the hands-on practical aspect of Microsoft word and how to improve your overall productivity with the hidden features embedded in Microsoft word. Without wasting any more time lets dive into the basic features of the application.

Getting Started: Exploring the Basic Features

we will explore the fundamental features of Microsoft Word that are essential for anyone who wants to use this software effectively.

First, we will cover the basics of creating and saving documents, including how to set up a new document, how to save it to your computer, and how to use the various formatting tools to make your document look professional.

Creating a New Document

1. Open Microsoft Word.
2. Click on the "File" tab in the top left corner of the screen.
3. Click on "New" to open a list of document templates.
4. Select the type of document you want to create (e.g., "Blank document" or "Resume").
5. Click on "Create" to open a new document.

Saving a Document

1. Click on the "File" tab in the top left corner of the screen.
2. Click on "Save As" to open the "Save As" dialog box.
3. Choose where you want to save the document by selecting a folder or location on your computer.
4. Type a name for the document in the "File name" field.
5. Choose the file format you want to save the document in (e.g., "Word Document" or "PDF" etc.).
6. Click on "Save" to save the document.

Congratulations! You are now skilled at using Microsoft Word to create new documents and save them. With the help of this robust word processing tool, you're well on your way to becoming a pro. But hold on, there's more to discover! Now it's time to tackle the challenge of formatting your text to suit your specific preferences. With the right tools and techniques, you'll be able to make your text stand out, convey your message more effectively, and impress readers by using the appropriate tools and strategies. Let's get started and learn how to improve your document formatting!

Text Formatting in Microsoft Word

In this section we are going to talk about formatting text, changing fonts, font size, indentation, paragraph spacing, styling etc.

Changing the Font Type and Size [Ctrl+Shift+F]

1. Select the text you want to format.
2. Click on the "Home" tab in the ribbon.
3. In the "Font" group, select the font type you want from the drop-down menu.
4. To change the font size, select the font size you want from the drop-down menu.

Changing the Font Styling

1. Select the text you want to format.
2. Click on the "Home" tab in the ribbon.
3. In the "Font" group, click on the "Bold," "Italic," or "Underline" button to apply the corresponding style.

Changing the Font Color and Highlight

1. Select the text you want to format.
2. Click on the "Home" tab in the ribbon.
3. In the "Font" group, click on the "Font Color" button to select a color for your text.
4. To apply a highlight color, click on the "Text Highlight Color" button and select the color you want.

Styles

Styles are predefined formatting options that allow users to quickly apply a consistent and professional look to their documents. These styles include font styles, font sizes, colors, paragraph spacing, and other formatting options that can be customized and saved for later use. Quick Styles are designed to save time and effort for users who want to create professional-looking documents without having to manually format each element individually.

Applying Styles to Text

1. Select the text you want to apply the style to.
2. In the "Styles" pane, click on the style you want to apply.

That's it! The selected text will now be formatted according to the style you selected.

Customizing Styles

In Microsoft Word, you have the option to personalize and create styles. This can help you work more efficiently by applying a particular style to multiple documents instead of manually changing the text every time. It saves you time and effort, allowing you to focus on your work without getting bogged down in formatting details. It's a handy feature that can make your life easier when using Microsoft Word.

Creating Custom Styles in Microsoft Word

1. Select the text that you want to use as a basis for your new style.
2. In the "Styles" pane, click on the "New Style" button.
3. In the "Create New Style from Formatting" dialog box, give your new style a name.
4. Choose the formatting characteristics you want to include in your new style.

5. Click on "OK" to save your new style.

Your new style will now be available in the "Styles" pane, and you can apply it to any text in your document.

Modifying Styles

1. If you want to modify an existing style in Microsoft Word, follow these steps:
2. In the "Styles" pane, right-click on the style you want to modify.
3. Select "Modify" from the context menu.
4. Make the changes you want to the style.
5. Click on "OK" to save your changes.

Your modified style will now be available in the "Styles" pane, and any text that has the style applied to it will be updated with the new formatting.

Removing Styles

If you want to remove a style from text in your document, follow these steps:

1. Select the text that has the style applied to it.
2. In the "Styles" pane, click on the "Clear Formatting" button.

The selected text will now be formatted using the default formatting for your document.

Copy Cut and Paste

Copy, cut, and paste are basic functions that allows you to duplicate or move text within a document or between different documents.

Copy: This allows a user to copy a selected text to clipboard while retaining the original text.

Cut: This allows a user to copy a selected text to clipboard without retaining the original text.

Paste: This allows a user to place a copied text into a selected location in a document.

Steps to Using Copy, Cut and Paste in Microsoft Word

1. Select the text you want to copy by highlighting it with your cursor.
2. Right-click on the highlighted text and select "Copy" or "Cut" from the context menu.
3. Navigate to the location where you want to paste the copied text.
4. Right-click and select "Paste" from the context menu, or use the keyboard shortcut Ctrl+V (Command+V on a Mac).
5. The copied text will appear at the new location.

The major difference between copy and cut is that copy duplicate a data while cut removes the original data.

Text Alignment

Text alignment is an important aspect of document formatting that can make your document look more polished and professional.

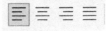

Alignment Types

In Microsoft Word, there are four types of text alignment options available: left-aligned, center-aligned, right-aligned, and justified.

14

Left-aligned [Ctrl + L]: This is the default alignment option in Word, where text is aligned along the left margin of the document, creating a clean and organized appearance. This is commonly used for body text in documents.

Center-aligned [Ctrl + E]: In this alignment, the text is centered on the page, creating a symmetrical look. This is often used for headings, titles, or other short lines of text.

Right-aligned [Ctrl + R]: This alignment option aligns text along the right margin of the document. It is useful for aligning numbers or other data along the right edge of a column, such as in tables or lists.

Justified [Ctrl + J]: In justified alignment, text is aligned to both the left and right margins of the document, creating a clean and polished appearance. This is commonly used for blocks of text, such as in newspaper or magazine columns.

Changing Text Alignment in Microsoft Word

1. Select the text you want to change the alignment
2. Click the alignment button in the "Paragraph" group of the "Home" tab in the ribbon depending on the choice of alignment.

Alternatively, you can use any of the shortcuts above to align your selected text

Bullets and Numbering

Bullets are small symbols or icons that can be applied to individual items in a list. They help to highlight each item and create a visual separation between them.

Numbering, on the other hand, automatically assigns sequential numbers or other symbols to items in a list. This is useful for creating ordered or hierarchical lists, such as step-by-step instructions or outlines.

Both bullet and numbering options can be customized in terms of style, indentation, and alignment to suit your document's formatting requirements. They provide a clear and structured way to present information, making it easier for readers to follow along and comprehend the content.

Adding bullet and numbering to a document

1. Select the text you want to add numbering to.
2. Click on the "Home" tab at the top of the screen.
3. In the "Paragraph" section, click on the "Numbering" or "Bullet" icon. A drop-down menu will appear, showing a variety of different numbering or bullet formats.
4. Choose the numbering or bullet format you want to use from the drop-down menu.
5. The selected text will now be formatted with the selected bullet or numbering system.
6. Custom Bullets and Numbering.

Creating a custom bullet:

1. Click on the "Home" tab at the top of the screen.
2. In the "Paragraph" section, click on the "Bullets" icon. A drop-down menu will appear, showing a variety of different bullet styles.
3. Scroll to the bottom of the list and select "Define New Bullet". The "Define New Bullet" dialog box will appear.
4. In the "Define New Bullet" dialog box, click on the "Symbol" button. This will open the "Symbol" dialog box.
5. In the "Symbol" dialog box, select the font that you want to use for your custom bullet.
6. Choose the symbol you want to use as your custom bullet by scrolling through the list of available symbols. You can also type a

specific character code in the "Character code" field to find a specific symbol.

7. Once you've selected your symbol, click "OK" to close the "Symbol" dialog box.
8. Back in the "Define New Bullet" dialog box, you can choose a font size, color, and alignment for your custom bullet.
9. Click "OK" to save your custom bullet.

Creating a custom numbering:

1. Click on the "Home" tab at the top of the screen.
2. In the "Paragraph" section, click on the "Numbering" icon. A drop-down menu will appear, showing a variety of different numbering formats.
3. Scroll to the bottom of the list and select "Define New Number Format". The "Define New Number Format" dialog box will appear.
4. In the "Define New Number Format" dialog box, you can choose a numbering style, such as Arabic or Roman numerals, and select the starting number for your list.
5. You can also add text before or after the number by typing it in the "Number format" field.
6. Click "OK" to save your custom numbering.

Find and Replace

The "Find and Replace" function in Microsoft Word is a widely used tool that enables you to locate specific text within your document and substitute it with different text. This powerful feature proves immensely time-saving, particularly when you have to make identical modifications in numerous sections of your document. Rather than manually editing each occurrence, "Find and Replace" streamlines the process, empowering you to swiftly and efficiently update your content with ease.

17

Using find and replace in Microsoft word

1. Open the document you want to search and replace text in.
2. Click on "Home" tab in the Ribbon.
3. Click on the "Replace" button in the "Editing" group. Alternatively, you can use the keyboard shortcut Ctrl+H.
4. In the "Find and Replace" dialog box, enter the text you want to find in the "Find what" field.
5. If you want to replace the text with something else, enter the new text in the "Replace with" field.
6. Click on the "Find Next" button to locate the first instance of the text you want to replace.
7. To replace the text, click on the "Replace" button. To replace all instances of the text, click on the "Replace All" button.
8. If you want to limit the search to specific parts of the document, such as headers or footers, click on the "More >>" button to expand the options and select the appropriate checkboxes.
9. Click on the "Close" button when you are finished replacing text.

Paragraph and indentation

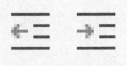

Paragraphs are a way of breaking up long blocks of text into smaller, more manageable chunks. In Microsoft Word, they are separated from one another by a blank line.

Indentation, on the other hand, is the amount of space between the left margin of a paragraph and the start of the text within it. Using indentation can help your document look more polished and organized, especially when used for quotes, lists, or new paragraphs. Paragraph can be created using the enter key

Manipulating Paragraph Indentation in Microsoft Word:

1. To adjust the indentation of your paragraph, select the paragraph(s) you want to change.
2. To increase the indentation, Click on the Increase Indent button on the home tab. This will add a half inch of space between the left margin and the text within the paragraph.
3. To decrease the indentation, click on the Decrease Indent button on the home tab. This will remove a half inch of space between the left margin and the text within the paragraph.

Custom Indentation

1. To apply a custom amount of indentation, click on the Paragraph Dialog Box Launcher (located in the Paragraph section of the home tab). This will open the Paragraph dialog box.
2. In the Paragraph dialog box, you can specify a precise indentation value (in inches) in the "Indentation" section.
3. You can also choose to indent the entire paragraph (Hanging) or just the first line (first line).
4. Click "OK" to apply the changes.

Working with Tables

Tables allows users to organize and present data in a structured and visually appealing way. A table consists of rows and columns, which can be used to create a variety of formats such as calendars, schedules, and lists. Tables can also be used to create more complex layouts, such as forms and invoices.

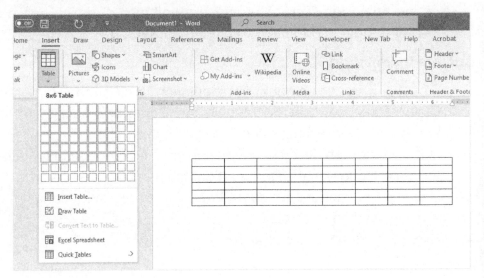

Creating a Table

1. Click on the "Insert" tab at the top of the screen.
2. In the "Tables" section, click on the "Table" icon. A drop-down menu will appear, allowing you to select the number of rows and columns you want in your table.
3. Click and drag your cursor over the grid to select the number of rows and columns you want. Alternatively, you can click on "Insert Table" and enter the number of rows and columns manually.
4. Click "OK" to create the table. It will appear in your document.

5. You can now customize your table by adding text, formatting cells, changing borders, etc.
6. To add text to a cell, simply click on the cell and begin typing.

Adding and Deleting Cells in a Table

Steps to inserting cells in a table

1. Click anywhere you want to insert cells within the table to select it.
2. Place your cursor in the cell where you want to add a new cell.
3. Right-click on the cell and select "Insert" from the context menu.
4. Choose whether you want to insert a new row or column. You can also choose to insert cells to the left or right of the selected cell, or above or below the selected cell.
5. Click "OK" to insert the new cells.

Alternatively, you can also add cells by clicking on the "Layout" tab in the ribbon, and then selecting "Insert Above" or "Insert Below" to add rows, or "Insert Left" or "Insert Right" to add columns.

Steps to deleting cells in a table

1. Click anywhere within the table to select it.
2. Place your cursor in the cell that you want to delete.
3. Right-click on the cell and select "Delete" from the context menu.
4. Choose whether you want to delete the entire row or column, or just the selected cell.
5. Click "OK" to delete the cell(s).

Alternatively, you can also delete cells by clicking on the "Layout" tab in the ribbon, and then selecting "Delete Rows" or "Delete Columns" to delete entire rows or columns, or "Delete Cells" to delete only the selected cells.

Merging and splitting Table cells

Merging and splitting help a user to combine two or more cells into one or split one cell into two or more.

Merging Cells

1. Select the cells you want to merge.
2. Right-click on the selected cells and click on "Merge Cells" in the context menu.
3. The selected cells will be merged into one cell.
4. Alternatively, you can also merge cells by selecting the cells, clicking on the "Layout" tab in the ribbon, and then clicking on "Merge Cells".

Splitting Cells

1. Place your cursor in the cell you want to split.
2. Click on the "Layout" tab in the ribbon.
3. Click on "Split Cells."
4. Choose the number of rows and columns you want to split the cell into.
5. Click "OK" to split the cell.
6. Alternatively, you can also split cells by selecting the cell, right-clicking on it, and then clicking on "Split Cells" in the context menu.

Sorting and filtering tables

Sorting enables users to quickly organize and analyze data in their tables. Sorting allows users to rearrange rows of data based on a particular column in either ascending or descending order. This can be especially useful when working with large tables of information, making it easier to find specific information or to analyze the data more effectively.

Filtering, on the other hand, allows users to display only specific rows of data that meet certain criteria. For example, users can filter a table to show only rows where a particular value appears in a certain column. This feature can help users narrow down their data and quickly find what they need.

Sorting a Table

1. Select the entire table or the columns you want to sort.
2. Click on the "Layout" tab in the ribbon.
3. Click on the "Sort" button.
4. Choose the column you want to sort by and select either "Ascending" or "Descending" order.
5. Click "OK" to sort the table.
6. Alternatively, you can also sort a table by right-clicking anywhere within the table, selecting "Sort" from the context menu, and following the same steps.

Filtering a Table

1. Select the entire table or the columns you want to filter.
2. Click on the "Layout" tab in the ribbon.
3. Click on the "Filter" button.
4. Click on the filter arrow next to the column you want to filter.
5. Choose the criteria you want to filter by and click "OK" to filter the table.
6. Alternatively, you can also filter a table by right-clicking anywhere within the table, selecting "Filter" from the context menu, and following the same steps.

Table formatting

Customizing the appearance of tables in Microsoft word is important as it makes our table more visually appealing and more organized.

Formatting Table Borders and Shading

1. Click anywhere within the table to select it.
2. Click on the "Design" tab in the ribbon.
3. In the "Table Styles" group, select a table style that you like.
4. To customize the table border, click on the "Borders" drop-down menu in the "Table Styles" group and select the line style, color, and width you want.
5. To customize the table shading, click on the "Shading" drop-down menu in the "Table Styles" group and select the color you want.

Adjusting Table Column Widths and Row Heights

1. Click anywhere within the table to select it.
2. Hover your cursor over the right border of the column you want to adjust until it turns into a double-sided arrow.
3. Click and drag the border to the desired width.
4. To adjust row height, hover your cursor over the bottom border of the row you want to adjust until it turns into a double-sided arrow.
5. Click and drag the border to the desired height.

Aligning Text Within Cells

1. Click anywhere within the table to select it.
2. Click on the "Layout" tab in the ribbon.
3. In the "Alignment" group, choose the text alignment you want, such as left, center, or right alignment.

Working with Graphics (Shapes)

Graphics can help users create more visually appealing and effective documents, making it easier to communicate information and ideas to their audience. In Microsoft word, users can add various types of graphics to their documents, including images, shapes, charts, and SmartArt. And in this section, we are going to be talking about everything related to graphics.

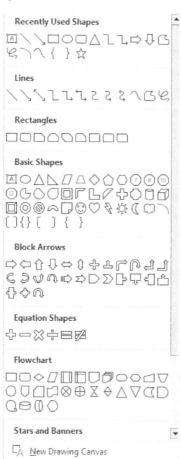

Shapes in Microsoft Word

Shapes are a type of graphic that allows users to add visual elements to their documents. Shapes can be used to create diagrams, flowcharts, and other visual aids that help illustrate key points and concepts.

Inserting Shapes in Microsoft Word

1. Click on the "Insert" tab at the top of the screen.
2. In the "Illustrations" section, click on the "Shapes" icon. A drop-down menu will appear, showing a variety of different shapes.
3. Select the shape you want to use by clicking on it. Your cursor will change to a crosshair.
4. Click and drag your cursor over the document to create the shape. The size and position of the shape can be adjusted by clicking and dragging its edges or corners.
5. To format the shape, click on it to select it, then click on the "Format" tab at the top of the screen.
6. Use the options in the "Shape Styles" section to change the color, outline, and effects of the shape.
7. To add text to the shape, click on it to select it, then begin typing.

Drawing Shapes in Microsoft Word

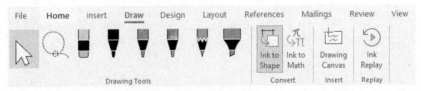

1. Select the Draw tab from the ribbon menu. If you can't see the Draw tab, right-click on any of the existing tabs and select Customize the Ribbon. From there, you can add the Draw tab to your ribbon.

2. Choose the type of shape you want to draw from the Shapes section. Word offers a variety of shapes, including lines, arrows, circles, rectangles, and more.
3. Click and drag your mouse on the document to draw the shape. You can adjust the size and shape of the shape by dragging the corners or edges.
4. Use the Draw tab tools to customize the shape. For example, you can use the Edit Points tool to adjust the shape of the line or curve, or use the Shape Styles tool to change the color and appearance of the shape.

Shape Formatting

Shape formatting is referred to as the customizing the appearance of shapes, such as changing their colors, outlines, sizes, and positions. With shape formatting, you can make your shapes stand out and match your document's style or design. By selecting a shape and using options in the Format tab, you can easily change its fill color, outline color, thickness, and even make it transparent. You can also resize and move shapes to fit your needs. Shape formatting allows you to create visually appealing and professional-looking documents with ease.

Shape Fill

Shape fill is a quick and simple way to add color and style to your shapes, making them stand out and enhancing the overall look of your document.

How to add fill colors to shapes

1. Click on the shape to select it.
2. Go to the "Format" tab in the menu bar.
3. In the "Shape Styles" group, click on the "Shape Fill" button.
4. Choose a fill option from the drop-down menu, such as a solid color, gradient, texture, or picture.

5. If you select a solid color, click on the desired color from the available options.
6. If you choose a gradient, select a gradient type and adjust the angle or direction if needed.
7. For a texture fill, choose a texture from the available options.
8. If you want to use a picture as a fill, select "Picture" from the fill options and browse for the desired image file on your computer.
9. Once you have selected the fill option, the shape will be filled accordingly.
10. Adjust the shape's fill settings, such as transparency or brightness, if desired.
11. Repeat these steps for any additional shapes you want to fill.
12. Save your document to preserve the changes you have made.

Shape Outline

Shape outline refers to the border or boundary that surrounds a shape. It defines the outer edges of the shape, providing a clear visual distinction between the shape and its surrounding content. The outline can be customized in terms of color, thickness, style, and transparency to suit your desired appearance. By adjusting the shape outline, you can enhance the visibility and aesthetics of the shape.

How to add outlines to Shapes

1. Select the shape you want to add an outline to.
2. Go to the "Format" tab in the menu bar.
3. Click on the "Shape Outline" button in the "Shape Styles" group.
4. Choose a color for the outline from the available options in the drop-down menu.
5. If desired, adjust the thickness of the outline by selecting an appropriate weight from the options.
6. To change the style of the outline, such as making it dashed or dotted, select the desired style from the options.

28

7. If you want to remove the outline, choose "No Outline" from the "Shape Outline" drop-down menu.
8. Repeat these steps for any additional shapes you want to add outlines to.

Shape Effect

Shapes effects refer to the various visual enhancements that can be applied to shapes to make them stand out or add a decorative element to the document. These effects allow you to customize the appearance of shapes by applying 3D effects, shadows, reflections, glows, bevels, and other visual enhancements.

By utilizing shape effects, you can add depth, realism, and visual interest to your shapes. These effects can be applied to individual shapes or multiple shapes collectively.

How to add effects to shapes

1. Select the shape you want to apply effects to.
2. Go to the "Format" tab in the menu bar.
3. Click on the "Shape Effects" button in the "Shape Styles" group.
4. From the drop-down menu, choose the desired effect category, such as "Shadow," "Reflection," "Glow," or "3D Format."
5. Select the specific effect you want to apply to the shape from the available options in the sub-menu.
6. Adjust the settings of the effect, such as the intensity, direction, size, or color, based on your preference.
7. To remove the effect, choose the "No Effect" option from the "Shape Effects" menu.
8. Repeat these steps for any additional shapes you want to apply effects to.

Shape Arrangement

Shapes arrangement refers to the positioning and alignment of multiple shapes in relation to each other. It allows you to organize and align shapes in a specific manner to create a well-structured and visually appealing layout.

To arrange shapes in Microsoft Word:

1. Select the shapes you want to arrange by clicking and dragging your mouse to draw a selection box around them, or hold down the "Shift" key and click on each shape individually.
2. Go to the "Format" tab in the menu bar.
3. In the "Arrange" group, you will find various options for arranging the selected shapes, such as "Align," "Distribute," and "Group."
4. Click on the "Align" button to access alignment options. Choose from options like aligning shapes to the left, right, center, top, bottom, or middle of the page or aligning them relative to each other.
5. Click on the "Distribute" button to access distribution options. These options allow you to evenly distribute the selected shapes horizontally or vertically.
6. To group shapes together, click on the "Group" button. This will combine the selected shapes into a single unit, making it easier to move and manipulate them as a group.
7. To ungroup shapes, select the grouped shape and click on the "Ungroup" button.
8. Adjust the position of individual shapes by clicking and dragging them to the desired location on the page.
9. Repeat these steps to further arrange and align other shapes in your document.
10. Save your document to preserve the changes.

Shape Alignment

Shapes alignment refers to the positioning of multiple shapes in a consistent and orderly manner, relative to each other or to the page. It allows you to ensure that shapes are evenly spaced, centered, or aligned along specific edges, creating a visually balanced and harmonious layout.

How to customize the alignment of shapes in Microsoft Word

1. Select the shapes you want to align by clicking and dragging your mouse to draw a selection box around them, or hold down the "Shift" key and click on each shape individually.
2. Go to the "Format" tab in the menu bar.
3. In the "Arrange" group, you will find various options for aligning the selected shapes, such as "Align Left," "Align Right," "Align Center," "Align Top," "Align Bottom," and more.
4. Click on the appropriate alignment button based on your desired outcome. For example, clicking on "Align Left" will align the left edges of the shapes, while clicking on "Align Center" will align the shapes based on their horizontal centers.
5. To distribute shapes evenly, click on the "Distribute Horizontally" or "Distribute Vertically" button. This will ensure equal spacing between the selected shapes.
6. To align shapes relative to each other, use the "Align to Margin" or "Align Selected Objects" options. This will align the shapes based on their relationship to the page margins or other selected objects.
7. Adjust the position of individual shapes by clicking and dragging them to the desired location on the page.
8. Repeat these steps to further align other shapes in your document.
9. Save your document to preserve the changes.

Word Art

Word Art in Microsoft Word refers to a feature that allows you to create stylized and decorative text. It enables you to apply various effects, such as different fonts, sizes, colors, and transformations, to make your text visually appealing and stand out in your documents.

How to add Word Art to a document in Microsoft Word:

1. Place your cursor in the document where you want to insert the Word Art.
2. Go to the "Insert" tab in the menu bar.
3. In the "Text" group, click on the "Word Art" button.
4. A drop-down menu will appear, showing different styles of Word Art. Choose the one that suits your needs or click on "More Word Art" to access additional options.
5. Click on the Word Art style you want to use. A text box will appear in your document, along with a new "Format" tab in the menu bar.
6. Type the desired text into the Word Art text box.
7. Use the "Format" tab to customize your Word Art. You can change the font, size, color, alignment, and other formatting options.
8. To apply additional effects, click on the "Text Effects" button in the "Word Art Styles" group. From there, you can add shadows, reflections, bevels, and other visual enhancements to your Word Art.
9. Adjust the position and size of the Word Art by clicking and dragging it to the desired location.
10. Save your document to preserve the changes.

Aligning and Distributing Shapes

Aligning and distributing shapes helps a user quickly change the positioning of multiple shapes at once by using the alignment and distribution options, which will save you time and effort.

How to align or distribute multiple shapes in Microsoft word

1.   Select all the shapes you want to align by holding down the Shift key and clicking on each shape.
2.   Click on the Format tab from the ribbon menu.
3.   In the Arrange group, click on the Align button. A drop-down menu will appear with various alignment options.
4.   Choose the alignment option you want to use, such as Align Left or Align Center.
5.   Repeat this process for the other alignment options, such as Align Right or Align Top.
6.   To distribute the shapes evenly, select all the shapes you want to distribute by holding down the Shift key and clicking on each shape.
7.   Click on the Format tab from the ribbon menu.
8.   In the Arrange group, click on the Align button and select Distribute Horizontally or Distribute Vertically.
9.   Your shapes should now be aligned and distributed according to your chosen options.

Grouping and Ungrouping Shapes

Steps to grouping Shapes in Microsoft word:

1.   Select all the shapes you want to group by holding down the Shift key and clicking on each shape.
2.   Right-click on one of the selected shapes and choose Group from the context menu.
3.   Click on Group again to confirm that you want to group the shapes.

33

4.   Your shapes are now grouped together and can be moved and resized as a single unit.

Steps to ungrouping Shapes in Microsoft word:

1.   Click on the grouped shape to select it.
2.   Right-click on the grouped shape and choose Group from the context menu.
3.   Click on Ungroup to separate the shapes.
4.   You may have to click Ungroup again to confirm that you want to ungroup the shapes.
5.   Your shapes are now ungrouped and can be moved and resized individually.

Layering Shapes

Controlling the order in which shapes appear on a page is made possible by shapes layering. There are different ways a shape can be layered. You can bring shapes to the front or send them to the back, or move them one layer forward or backward to create the desired effect. Layering shapes is particularly useful when working with complex designs or illustrations.

How to layer shapes in Microsoft word

1.   Click on the shape that you want to change the layer.
2.   From the Format tab, click on the Bring Forward or Send Backward button in the Arrange group.
3.   If you want to move the shape one layer forward or backward, click on the Bring Forward One Layer or Send Backward One Layer button respectively.
4.   If you want to bring the shape all the way to the front or move it all the way to the back, click on the Bring to Front or Send to Back button respectively.

5. If you want to layer multiple shapes, select the shapes you want to layer by holding down the Shift key and clicking on each shape.
6. From the Format tab, click on the Bring Forward or Send Backward button to arrange the shapes in the desired order.
7. Repeat this process until you have arranged all the shapes in the desired order.

Working with Images

Images play a crucial role in enhancing the visual appeal and overall effectiveness of documents. They allow users to incorporate graphical elements such as photographs, illustrations, diagrams, and charts into their written content. Images can effectively convey information, provide visual explanations, and engage the reader's attention. Microsoft word provides various features for handling images, such as resizing, cropping, and positioning, which enable users to fine-tune their appearance within the document.

Inserting Images

1. Create a new document in Microsoft Word.
2. Place your cursor at the location in the document where you want to insert the image.
3. On the top menu, click on the "Insert" tab.
4. In the "Insert" tab, you will find the "Pictures" button in the "Illustrations" group. Click on it.
5. A file explorer window will appear. Browse your computer's folders to locate the image file you want to insert. Select the image file and click the "Insert" button.
6. The selected image will be inserted into your document at the cursor's position.

Resizing Images

The ability to resize images is incredibly useful as it allows users to fit images seamlessly into their documents, ensuring they align with the overall layout and design. By adjusting the size of images, one can effectively control the visual impact they have on the reader, making them more visually appealing and balanced within the text. Additionally, resizing images allows users to shrink or enlarge images to better fit the available area without sacrificing clarity or quality. *How to resize images in Microsoft Word*

1. Click on the image to select it. You will notice small squares or handles on the corners and sides of the image.
2. Click and drag any of these handles to adjust the image's size proportionally. As you drag, you will see the image dimensions changing.
3. To maintain the image's original aspect ratio (proportions), hold down the Shift key on your keyboard while dragging the handles. This ensures that the image doesn't become distorted.
4. To resize the image without maintaining the aspect ratio, simply click and drag one of the corner handles without holding the Shift key. This allows you to stretch or squeeze the image in one direction.
5. As you resize the image, the surrounding text may adjust automatically to accommodate the changes. However, if you want more control over how the text wraps around the image, right-click on the image and select "Wrap Text." Choose an appropriate text wrapping option such as "Square," "Tight," or "Behind Text" from the context menu.
6. You can also manually adjust the position of the resized image by clicking on it and dragging it to the desired location within the document.
7. If you need precise control over the image's size, you can right-click on the image and select "Format Picture" from the context

menu. In the "Format Picture" pane or dialog box that appears, navigate to the "Size" tab. Here, you can enter specific values for height and width, or adjust the percentage scaling to resize the image accurately.

8. Once you are satisfied with the resized image, save your document to retain the changes.

Background Removal in Images

1. Click on the image to select it. This will reveal the "Picture Tools" tab at the top of the Word window.

2. Click on the "Picture Tools" tab, and within it, you will find the "Format" tab.

3. In the "Format" tab, locate the "Remove Background" button. It is usually found in the "Adjust" group.

4. Click on the "Remove Background" button. Word will automatically attempt to identify the background and highlight it with a purple overlay.

5. A "Background Removal" tab will appear on the Ribbon, providing you with additional options to fine-tune the background removal process.

6. On the "Background Removal" tab, you will see a set of tools and commands that allow you to modify the selected area further.

7. Use the "Mark Areas to Keep" and "Mark Areas to Remove" options in the "Background Removal" tab to refine the selection. Click and drag the cursor over the areas you want to keep or remove respectively.

8. Word will instantly update the preview, removing or retaining the marked areas based on your selection.

9. If necessary, you can adjust the selection using the handles and refine the result until you are satisfied.

10. Once you are content with the background removal, click outside the image to deselect it.

11. Save your document to retain the changes made to the image.

Picture Styles

Picture styles are predefined visual effects that can be applied to images within a document. These styles allow users to quickly and easily enhance the appearance of their images without the need for advanced editing skills. Picture styles include various combinations of borders, shadows, reflections, glows, and other effects that can be applied to images with just a few clicks.

How to apply picture styles to images

1. Click on the image to select it. The "Picture Tools" tab will appear at the top of the Word window.

2. Click on the "Picture Tools" tab. Within this tab, you will find the "Format" tab.

3. In the "Format" tab, locate the "Picture Styles" group. It contains a variety of predefined styles that you can apply to the selected image.

4. Click on the small arrow icon in the bottom right corner of the "Picture Styles" group. This will open the "Format Picture" pane or dialog box, depending on your Word version.

5. In the "Format Picture" pane or dialog box, navigate to the "Picture Styles" tab.

6. Browse through the available picture styles. You will see a live preview of each style applied to the image as you hover over them.

7. Click on the desired picture style to apply it to the selected image. Word will instantly update the image's appearance with the chosen style.

8. To further customize the picture style, you can use the options in the "Format Picture" pane or dialog box. Adjustments may include modifying the border, shadow, reflection, glow, or other effects associated with the selected style.

9. Keep experimenting with different picture styles until you find the one that best suits your image and document's overall look and feel.

10. Once you are satisfied with the applied picture style, close the "Format Picture" pane or dialog box.

Color Variations in Images

Color variation in images in Microsoft Word refers to the ability to adjust and modify the colors of an image within the document. With the available tools and options, users can enhance or change the saturation, brightness, contrast, and other aspects of the image's color

How to customize the color of an image

1. Click on the image to select it. This will reveal the "Picture Tools" tab at the top of the Word window.

2. Click on the "Picture Tools" tab, and within it, you will find the "Format" tab.

3. In the "Format" tab, locate the "Color" group. This group contains various options for adjusting the color of the selected image.

4. Click on the small arrow icon in the bottom right corner of the "Color" group. This will open the "Format Picture" pane or dialog box, depending on your Word version.

5. In the "Format Picture" pane or dialog box, navigate to the "Color" tab.

6. On the "Color" tab, you will find different options to adjust the color variations of the image. These options may include "Saturation," "Brightness," "Contrast," and others, depending on your Word version.

7. Adjust the desired color variations by moving sliders or entering values in the corresponding fields. As you make adjustments, you will see the image's color change in real time.

8. Explore the available options to achieve the desired color effect. For example, you can increase or decrease the saturation to make the colors more vibrant or muted, adjust the brightness to make the image brighter or darker, or modify the contrast to enhance or reduce the difference between light and dark areas.

9. Once you are satisfied with the color variations, close the "Format Picture" pane or dialog box.

10. Save your document to retain the changes made to the image.

Image Positioning

Image positioning enables a user to control the placement and alignment of images within a document. Users can choose from various options like in-line with text, behind or in front of text, or wrap text around the image. By adjusting the positioning, users can create a visually appealing layout, control the flow of text around the image, and enhance the document's overall design. Precise image positioning allows for better integration of visuals with the surrounding content, ensuring a professional and polished appearance.

Customizing Image position in Microsoft Word

1. Click on the image to select it. This will reveal the "Picture Tools" tab at the top of the Word window.

2. Click on the "Picture Tools" tab, and within it, you will find the "Format" tab.

3. In the "Format" tab, locate the "Arrange" group. This group contains options for positioning and aligning the selected image.

4. Click on the "Position" button within the "Arrange" group. A drop-down menu will appear with various positioning options.

5. Choose the desired positioning option from the menu. The available options may include "In Line with Text," "Square," "Tight," "Through," "Behind Text," "In Front of Text," and more.

6. If you select "In Line with Text," the image will be positioned as part of the text flow. You can then adjust its placement by dragging it to the desired location within the document.

7. For more precise positioning, click on the "Wrap Text" button within the "Arrange" group. This will open a drop-down menu with additional text wrapping options.

8. Select the desired text wrapping option from the menu, such as "Tight," "Through," or "Top and Bottom." These options allow you to control how the text wraps around the image.

9. Once you have chosen the positioning and text wrapping options, adjust the image's placement by clicking and dragging it to the desired location within the document.

10. To fine-tune the image's position, you can use the arrow keys on your keyboard to move the image pixel by pixel.

11. Save your document to retain the changes made to the image positioning.

Crop, Rotate and Arrange

Crop

1. Click on the image to select it. This will reveal the "Picture Tools" tab at the top of the Word window.

2. Click on the "Picture Tools" tab, and within it, you will find the "Format" tab.

3. In the "Format" tab, locate the "Adjust" group. This group contains options for cropping, rotating, and arranging the selected image.

4. To crop the image, click on the "Crop" button in the "Adjust" group. This will display crop handles around the image.

5. Click and drag the crop handles to select the portion of the image you want to keep. The area outside the selected portion will be cropped out. To fine-tune the crop, use the crop handles on the sides and corners of the image.

6. Once you are satisfied with the cropping, press the "Enter" key on your keyboard or click outside the image to apply the crop.

Rotate and Arrange

1. To rotate the image, click on the "Rotate" button in the "Adjust" group. Choose from the options to rotate the image clockwise or counterclockwise by specific degrees or flip it horizontally or vertically.

2. If you want to arrange the image in relation to the text, click on the "Wrap Text" button in the "Arrange" group. Choose the desired text wrapping option, such as "In Line with Text," "Square," or "Behind Text." This will determine how the text flows around the image.

3. To position the image precisely, click and drag it to the desired location within the document.

4. Save your document to retain the changes made to the image.

Image Transparency

1. Click on the image to select it. This will reveal the "Picture Tools" tab at the top of the Word window.

2. Click on the "Picture Tools" tab, and within it, you will find the "Format" tab.

3. In the "Format" tab, locate the "Adjust" group. This group contains options for adjusting the image's appearance, including transparency.

4. Click on the "Artistic Effects" button within the "Adjust" group. This will open a drop-down menu with various artistic effects and adjustments.

5. At the bottom of the drop-down menu, click on the "Picture Effects Options" button. This will open the "Format Picture" pane or dialog box, depending on your Word version.

6. In the "Format Picture" pane or dialog box, navigate to the "Picture" or "Effects" tab.

7. Look for the "Transparency" or "Opacity" slider. By moving the slider, you can increase or decrease the transparency of the selected image.

8. Adjust the transparency to your desired level by dragging the transparency slider or entering a specific value.

9. As you make adjustments, you will see the image's transparency change in real time, allowing you to preview the effect.

10. Once you are satisfied with the transparency, close the "Format Picture" pane or dialog box.

11. Save your document to retain the changes made to the image's transparency.

Alt Text

1. Right-click on the image and select "Edit Alt Text" from the context menu. This will open the "Alt Text" pane on the right side of the Word window.

2. In the "Alt Text" pane, you will see a text box labeled "Description." This is where you can enter the ALT text for the image.

3. Type a concise and descriptive summary of the image in the "Description" text box. The ALT text should provide a clear and meaningful description of the image's content or function.

4. If needed, you can also provide additional information or context in the "Title" field within the "Alt Text" pane. However, the "Title" field is optional and not always necessary.

5. Once you have entered the ALT text and, if desired, the title, close the "Alt Text" pane.

6. Save your document to retain the ALT text for the image.

Captions

Captions refer to the descriptive text that accompanies images, tables, or other objects within a document. They provide context and help readers understand the content or purpose of the visual element. With captions, users can effectively label and explain visual elements, ensuring a clear and informative reading experience.

Adding Captions to an Image in Microsoft Word

1. Click on the object to select it.
2. Go to the "References" tab at the top of the Word window. This tab contains tools for managing captions.

3. Within the "References" tab, locate the "Captions" group. It includes options for adding and customizing captions.
4. Click on the "Insert Caption" button within the "Captions" group. A dialog box titled "Caption" will appear.
5. In the "Caption" dialog box, enter the desired caption text in the "Caption" text box. This should provide a brief and descriptive summary of the object.
6. Choose the desired label from the "Label" drop-down menu. The label identifies the type of object, such as "Figure," "Table," or "Equation." You can also create custom labels by selecting "New Label" from the drop-down menu.
7. If you want the captions to be numbered sequentially, ensure that the "Include chapter number" or "Include label and number" option is selected, depending on your preference.
8. Customize the position of the caption by selecting the desired option from the "Position" drop-down menu. Options may include "Above selected item" or "Below selected item."
9. If you wish to change the formatting of the caption, click on the "Format" button in the "Caption" dialog box. This will allow you to modify font, size, style, and other formatting options.
10. Click the "OK" button to insert the caption. The caption will appear near the selected object.
11. Save your document to retain the added caption.

Smart Arts

SmartArt is a feature that allows you to create professional-looking diagrams and graphics quickly and easily. SmartArt graphics are pre-built templates that you can customize to suit your needs. They can be used for a wide range of purposes, including flowcharts, organization charts, timelines, and process diagrams. I will walk you through how to include and format SmartArt in your Word document.

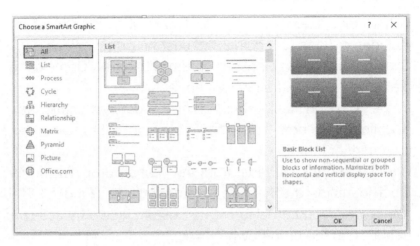

Including SmartArt in a Word Document

1. Click on the Insert tab in the ribbon.
2. Click on the SmartArt button in the Illustrations group. The SmartArt graphic gallery will open.
3. Choose the type of SmartArt graphic you want to use from the gallery. You can choose from categories such as List, Process, Hierarchy, Relationship, Matrix, and Pyramid.
4. Click on the SmartArt graphic you want to use and click the OK button. The SmartArt graphic will be inserted into your document.

Formatting SmartArt in a Word Document

1. After inserting the SmartArt graphic, it will be selected by default. If not, click on the graphic to select it.
2. The Design and Format tabs will appear in the ribbon. These tabs allow you to customize your SmartArt graphic with various formatting options.
3. To change the layout of the SmartArt graphic, select the graphic and click on the Layouts button in the Design tab. Choose the layout you want to use from the gallery.

4. To change the color of the SmartArt graphic, select the graphic and click on the Change Colors button in the SmartArt Styles group in the Design tab. Choose the color scheme you want to use from the gallery.
5. To add or remove shapes in the SmartArt graphic, select the graphic and click on the Add Shape or Remove Shape button in the SmartArt Tools group in the Design tab.
6. To add or edit text in the SmartArt graphic, select the graphic and click inside the text boxes. Type in your text or edit the existing text as desired.
7. To resize the SmartArt graphic, select the graphic and drag the sizing handles in or out to adjust the size as desired.
8. To move the SmartArt graphic, select the graphic and drag it to a new location in your document.

Booyah! You have successfully completed this section of the Microsoft Word tutorial. By now, you should have a good understanding of the fundamental features of Word, including creating, saving, and editing documents, formatting text, working with tables and graphics, and using various tools such as shapes and SmartArt.

Advanced Features of Microsoft Word

We are going to be moving up further into the advanced topics of Microsoft word and In this Chapter, we will be diving into topics related to Page Structure and customization (margins, themes, borders, headers, footers, numbering etc.). So, hold on tight as we go for a ride in the outer space.

Page Layout, Structure and Customization

Page layout and structure refers to the arrangement and design of text, images, and other elements on a page or document. This includes setting margins, adjusting page orientation, adding headers and footers, creating columns, and other formatting options that affect the overall look and feel of the document. The page layout and structure can greatly impact the readability and overall effectiveness of the document, making it important to consider when creating or editing a document in Word.

Selecting a page size in Microsoft word

1. Click on the "Layout" tab in the Ribbon menu.
2. In the "Page Setup" section, click on the "Size" dropdown menu to see a list of preset paper sizes.
3. Select the desired paper.
4. Select the desired orientation under "Orientation" in the "Page Setup" section.
5. Click "OK" to apply the changes.

Customizing Page Size and Orientation

A custom page size allows a user to have authority over a page height, width, margins etc. depending on the user's preference.

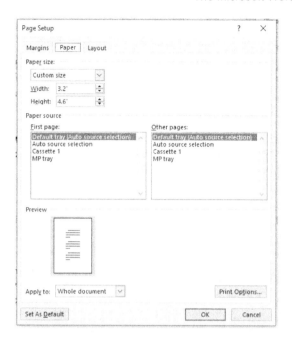

Creating a Custom Page Size

1. Click on the "Layout" tab in the Ribbon menu at the top of the screen.

2. In the "Page Setup" section, click on the small arrow in the bottom-right corner to open the "Page Setup" dialog box.

3. In the "Page Setup" dialog box, select the "Paper" tab.

4. Under the "Paper Size" section, select the "Custom Size" option.

5. Enter the desired width and height for your custom page size in the "Width" and "Height" fields, respectively. You can choose to enter the values in inches, centimeters, or millimeters.

6. If necessary, select the "Portrait" or "Landscape" orientation option under the "Orientation" section.

7. Under the "Margins" section, adjust the margins as necessary for your custom page size. You can choose to set margins for the entire document or specify different margins for different sections.

8. Click on the "OK" button to apply your custom page size to the document.

9. If you want to save the custom page size for future use, click on the "Paper" tab again in the "Page Setup" dialog box.
10. Under the "Paper Size" section, click on the "Save" button.
11. Give the custom page size a name that you will remember and click "OK" to save it.
12. Your custom page size will now be available to select from the "Size" dropdown menu under the "Page Setup" section in the "Layout" tab.

Margins

Margins refer to the space between the edge of the paper and the content of your document. In Microsoft Word, you can adjust the margins to control the amount of white space on the top, bottom, left, and right sides of your document.

Customizing margins in Microsoft word

1. Click on the "Layout" tab at the top of the screen.
2. Click on "Margins" and a dropdown menu will appear with different margin options.
3. Select the margin size that you want to use, or click on "Custom Margins" to create your own.
4. If you choose "Custom Margins," enter your desired margin size for the top, bottom, left, and right sides of the document.
5. Click "OK" to save your changes.

Page Breaks

Page break is a tool used in word processing to control the placement of content on a page. In Microsoft Word, a page break is used to split content between pages, ensuring that text and images do not overlap or spill over into the next page. You can insert a page break at any point in your document to start a new page or to control the layout of your content.

Inserting page breaks in Microsoft word

1. Click where you want to insert a page break.
2. Click on the "Insert" tab at the top of the screen.
3. Click on "Page Break" in the "Pages" group, and a new blank page will be inserted at the cursor location.
4. To remove a page break, place your cursor just before the page break and press the "Delete" key on your keyboard.

Alternatively, you can use the "Breaks" option in the "Page Setup" group under the "Layout" tab to insert different types of breaks, such as section breaks, column breaks, and even page breaks with specific formatting.

Themes

Themes are predefined collections of colors, fonts, and effects that you can apply to your document to give it a consistent and professional look. Applying a theme can quickly change the appearance of your document without having to manually adjust individual elements.

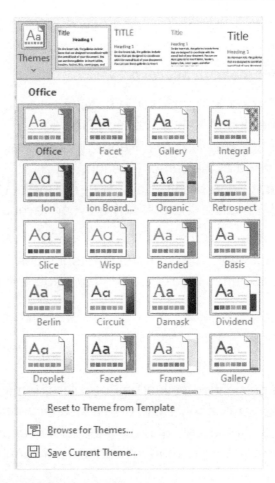

Applying a theme in Microsoft word

1. Click on the "Design" tab on the ribbon at the top of the screen.
2. Browse through the different theme options to find one that you like.
3. Click on the theme to apply it to your document.
4. Once you have applied the theme, you can further customize it by clicking on the "Themes" dropdown menu and selecting "Theme Options."
5. From the Theme Options menu, you can adjust the colors, fonts, and effects to match your specific needs.

6. If you want to remove the theme from your document, simply click on the "Design" tab and select "No Theme" from the dropdown menu.

Backgrounds in Microsoft word

1. Click on the "Design" tab on the ribbon at the top of the screen.
2. Click on the "Page Color" dropdown menu to select a background color or choose "Fill Effects" to customize your background.
3. In the "Fill Effects" menu, you can choose from various options, such as gradients, patterns or textures.
4. To create a custom background, select the "Picture" tab to choose a picture as your background. You can choose from preloaded images or select "From File" to upload your own image.
5. Once you have selected an image, you can adjust its appearance by selecting "Picture Corrections" or "Picture Effects" from the dropdown menu.
6. You can also adjust the placement of your background image by selecting "Wrap Text" from the dropdown menu and choosing a placement option.
7. If you want to remove the background, simply click on the "Page Color" dropdown menu and select "No Color."

Page Borders

Page borders are decorative lines that can be added to the pages of a document to enhance its appearance. They can be used to frame text, images, or other page elements.

Adding page borders to a Microsoft word document

1. Click on the "Page Layout" tab in the ribbon.
2. Click on the "Page Borders" button, which is located in the "Page Background" group.

3. In the "Borders and Shading" dialog box, select the "Page Border" tab.
4. Choose the type of border you want to use from the "Setting" section. You can choose from options such as "Box," "Shadow," or "3-D."
5. Customize the border style, color, and width using the options in the "Style," "Color," and "Width" sections.
6. Select the "Apply to" drop-down menu and choose where you want to apply the border. You can choose to apply it to the whole document, a section of the document, or just the current section.
7. Click the "OK" button to apply the border to your document.
8. You can also add page borders using the "Art" tab in the "Borders and Shading" dialog box. This tab contains a collection of pre-designed borders that you can choose from. To use one of these borders, simply select it from the list and customize it as needed.

Headers and Footers

A header is a section of a document that appears at the top of each page, while a footer is a section of a document that appears at the bottom of each page. Headers and footers can contain text, images, page numbers, and other information that should be consistent across all pages of the document.

Adding Header and Footer to a Document

1. Click on the "Insert" tab.
2. Click on the "Header" or "Footer" button, depending on which one you want to add.
3. Select one of the pre-designed header or footer options, or click on "Edit Header" or "Edit Footer" to create a custom one.
4. Type in the text or information you want to include in the header or footer. You can also insert graphics, such as a company logo.

5. To customize the header or footer, click on the "Design" tab that appears when you're working within the header or footer section. Here you can choose from various styles, colors, and fonts to make your header or footer stand out.
6. If you want to add page numbers to your header or footer, click on the "Page Number" button and select the style you prefer.
7. Once you're satisfied with your header or footer, click on the "Close Header and Footer" button to return to the main document.

Page Numbering

Page Numbering is assigning numbers to the pages of a document. It helps readers find specific information and maintains a professional appearance. In Microsoft Word, authors of a document can easily add page numbers using built-in features.

1. Click on the Insert tab on the ribbon at the top of the window.
2. Click on the Page Number dropdown menu, located on the right side of the ribbon.
3. Choose the position and style of page numbering that you want to use. Options include top of page, bottom of page, and margins.
4. After selecting the desired option, choose a specific page numbering style from the available options. You can also customize the numbering format if you wish.
5. Once you have selected the desired page numbering style, it will be applied to all pages in your document.
6. If you want to customize page numbering on specific pages (for example, starting with a different number on the second page), double-click on the header or footer of the page where you want to make changes.
7. In the header or footer section, click on the Page Number dropdown menu and select the "Format Page Numbers" option.

8. In the Format Page Numbers dialog box, you can choose to start page numbering at a specific number or format the numbers differently on certain pages.
9. Click OK to save your changes and exit the dialog box.
10. Repeat steps 6-9 for any additional pages where you want to customize page numbering.

Columns

Columns are used to divide a page into separate sections, allowing you to structure text and other elements in a more visually appealing manner.

Adding columns into your Microsoft word document

1. Click on the Page Layout tab in the ribbon at the top of the screen.
2. In the Page Setup section, click on the Columns dropdown menu.
3. Select the number of columns you want to add to your document. You can choose from one, two, three, or more columns.
4. If you want to customize the width of your columns, click on More Columns at the bottom of the dropdown menu.
5. In the Columns dialog box, you can adjust the width and spacing of your columns, as well as add a line between them.
6. Click OK to apply your changes.

Document Organization

In this Chapter, we will be talking about everything related to the organization of documents for ease of access (Table of contents, hyperlinks, navigation pane, cross references, mailing and mail merge).

Document navigation and organization in Microsoft Word deals with how various parts of a document are accessed and arranged to make it easier to navigate and read. Proper document organization is essential for creating a professional-looking document that effectively communicates the intended message to the reader.

Effective document organization involves using various formatting and organizational tools available in Microsoft Word to create a document that looks professional, easy to navigate, and easy to understand.

Table of Contents

A table of contents is a list that appears at the beginning of a document and provides a quick reference for readers to navigate to specific sections or chapters in the document.

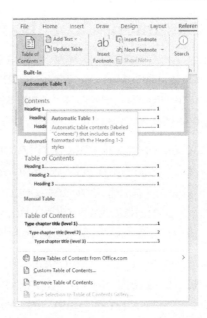

Adding Table of Contents to your Microsoft Word Document

Format your document headings: To create a table of contents, you need to use the heading styles to organize your content according to the headings (titles) and sub-headings. The different levels of headings should be formatted consistently, such as Heading 1, Heading 2, and Heading 3.

1. Place the cursor where you want to insert the table of contents: Typically, it is placed at the beginning of the document after the cover page.
2. Click on the References tab: This tab contains the tools necessary for creating a table of contents.
3. Click on the Table of Contents button: In the Table of Contents group, click on the Table of Contents button. A dropdown menu appears with several pre-formatted styles for you to choose from.
4. Select the style you want to use: Select the table of contents style that best matches your document's design and layout.
5. Customize your table of contents: If you want to make changes to the table of contents, such as adding or removing headings or

changing the style, click on the Table of Contents button again and select "Custom Table of Contents." Here you can select which headings to include, change the format, and more.

Update the table of contents: After you have made changes to your document, such as adding or deleting headings, it is important to update the table of contents. Click on the table of contents, then click on the "Update Table" button to update the content and page numbers.

Hyperlinks

Hyperlinks is a tool used for creating interactive and easy-to-navigate documents. They allow users to quickly access related information within the same document or to external sources such as websites or email addresses.

Adding Hyperlinks to your Microsoft Word Document

1. Highlight the text or image you want to turn into a hyperlink.
2. Click on the "Insert" tab in the top menu.
3. Click on the "link" option in the "Links" section.
4. In the "Insert Hyperlink" dialog box, select the type of link you want to create (e.g., website or email).
5. Enter the URL or email address you want to link to in the "Address" field.
6. Optionally, enter a description for the hyperlink in the "Text to display" field.
7. Click "OK" to create the hyperlink.
8. To edit or remove a hyperlink, simply right-click on the link and select the appropriate option from the context menu.

Footnotes

Footnotes in Microsoft Word refer to small notes or explanations placed at the bottom of a page. They are typically used to provide additional information, citations, or comments that are relevant to specific text within the document.

With footnotes, A user can expand on certain points in a document without interrupting the flow of the main text. For example when readers encounter a superscript number or symbol in the main text, they can refer to the corresponding footnote at the bottom of the page to access the additional information or citation.

Adding footnotes in Microsoft word

1. Open your document in Microsoft Word.
2. Place your cursor at the end of the sentence or word where you want to insert a footnote.
3. In the menu bar at the top, click on the "References" tab.
4. Within the "References" tab, locate the "Footnotes" section. Click on the "Insert Footnote" button.
5. A small superscript number will appear at the insertion point in the text, and the cursor will move to the bottom of the page.
6. At the bottom of the page, below the main text, you will find the newly created footnote area. Type your footnote text here.
7. To return to the main text, either click on the main body of the document or press the "Esc" key.
8. Your footnote will now be displayed at the bottom of the page, and the superscript number in the main text will correspond to it.
9. Repeat these steps for any additional footnotes you want to add.

Navigation Pane

The Navigation Pane is a tool that allows users to quickly and easily navigate through their document's contents. It provides an overview of the document structure, including headings, pages, sections, and other elements which make it easier for a user to move through the document.

How to enable and use the navigation pane in Microsoft word

1. Click on the "View" tab in the top menu.
2. Check the "Navigation Pane" option in the "Show" section. The Navigation Pane will appear on the left side of the screen.
3. Use the search bar at the top of the Navigation Pane to search for specific words or phrases in your document.
4. Click on any heading in the Navigation Pane to jump to that section of the document.
5. Click on the arrows next to each heading to expand or collapse its subsections.
6. Drag and drop headings in the Navigation Pane to reorganize your document's structure.
7. Right-click on a heading to access additional options, such as "Promote" or "Demote" headings, or "Delete" a section.

8. Use the "Show Heading Levels" drop-down menu at the top of the Navigation Pane to customize the level of detail displayed.
9. To close the Navigation Pane, simply uncheck the "Navigation Pane" option in the "View" tab.

Cross References

Cross references allow you to refer to a specific item or text in a document, such as a figure or heading, and create a link to that item. This feature can be very useful for navigation when creating complex or lengthy documents.

Adding and enabling cross references in your Microsoft word document

1. Insert the item you want to cross-reference. This could be a heading, figure, table, or any other item that you want to refer to in your document.
2. Place your cursor where you want to insert the cross-reference.
3. From the "References" tab in the ribbon, find the captions section and click "Cross-reference".
4. In the "Reference type" section, choose the type of item you want to reference, such as a heading or figure.
5. In the "Insert reference to" section, choose the specific item you want to reference.
6. In the "For which heading" section, choose the heading level you want to use, if applicable.
7. Click "Insert" to insert the cross-reference into your document.
8. Once you've inserted a cross-reference, you can also update it if necessary by right-clicking on the reference and selecting "Update field". This will ensure that the reference accurately reflects the item it is linked to. You can also customize the formatting of cross-

references using the "Insert reference to" section, such as changing the number format or adding a prefix or suffix.

Mailing and Mail Merge

Mailing is a unique feature that enables users to send personalized emails, letters, or labels to a large group of people. Whether you need to send invitations to an event or a newsletter to your clients, Microsoft Word has all the tools you need to get the job done quickly and efficiently. With its intuitive interface and powerful tools, mailing in Microsoft Word can save you time and effort while ensuring that your communication is professional and effective.

Mail Merge on the other hand is a feature that allows users to automate the process of creating personalized documents or emails by pulling data from a database or spreadsheet. It can save a lot of time and effort when sending mass emails or letters to different recipients. With Mail Merge, you can easily create a set of documents, each with personalized information, without having to manually input data for each document.

There are some configurations needed to be completed to be able to use Microsoft word for sending personalized documents.

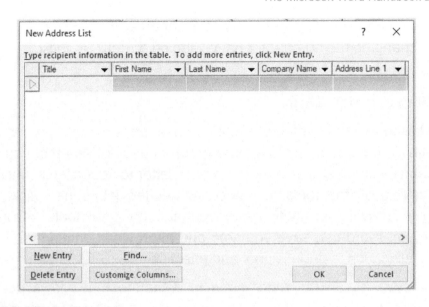

Creating Data Source

A data source is a file that contains information, such as names and addresses, that can be used to create a mail merge or form letter.

How to set up a data source in Microsoft word

1. Click on the "Mailings" tab.
2. In the "Start Mail Merge" group, click "Select Recipients" and choose "Type New List".
3. In the "New Address List" dialog box, choose the type of information you want to store in your data source, such as "Customize Columns".
4. In the "Customize Columns" dialog box, add the fields you want to include in your data source.
5. Fill in the information for each record in your data source.
6. Save the file with a name that is easy to remember and locate.
7. Once you have created your data source, you can use it to create a mail merge or form letter.

Inserting Merge Fields

Merge fields serve as placeholders for the variable (personalized) data that will be inserted into the final document.

Inserting merge fields in Microsoft word

1. Open the document that you want to insert merge fields into and place your cursor in the location where you want to insert merge fields.
2. Click on the "Mailings" tab in the ribbon.
3. Click on the "Select Recipients" button in the "Start Mail Merge" section.
4. Select Type a new list or select existing List. After selecting a list
5. Click on the "Insert Merge Field" button in the "Write & Insert Fields" section.
6. In the "Insert Merge Field" dialog box, select the merge field that you want to insert and click "Insert".
7. Repeat steps 4-6 for each merge field that you want to insert into your document.

Previewing Merge Fields

Previewing and editing merged documents allows you to see how the final merged document will look before printing or sending.

How to preview merged fields in Microsoft word

1. Open your merged document.
2. Click on the "Mailings" tab at the top of the screen.
3. Click on the "Preview Results" button in the "Preview" group.
4. This will switch to the "Preview Results" view, which shows how each individual record will look once merged.
5. Use the "Next" and "Previous" buttons to navigate through the records.

6.   Use the "Find a recipient" field to search for a specific record by keyword.
7.   If you notice any errors with a particular document, Go to the "Finish & Merge" group in the 'Finish' section and click on "Edit Individual Documents".
8.   In the "Merge to New Document" dialog box, select "All" to edit all records, or "Current record" to edit only the current record.
9.   Once you've made your edits, save the document.

Completing Document Merge

1.   After inserting the merge fields and previewing the merged data, click the "Finish & Merge" button in the "Finish" group on the "Mailings" tab.
2.   In the dropdown menu, choose the type of merged document you want to create, such as "Print Documents" or "Send Email Messages."
3.   If you selected "Print Documents," you can choose to print all the records or a specific range, as well as choose to edit individual documents before printing.
4.   If you selected "Send Email Messages," you can customize the email subject and message, and preview the emails before sending them.
5.   You may be prompted to save the merged document before printing or sending.

Collaboration in Microsoft Word

Collaboration is a feature in Microsoft word that allows multiple users to work together on a single document. By using features such as real-time co-authoring, comments, and track changes, teams can streamline their workflows and improve productivity. Microsoft Word also integrates with other Microsoft Office applications, such as Excel and PowerPoint, to enable cross-functional collaboration.

Sharing and Co-authoring

Co-authoring is a feature that enables multiple users to collaborate on the same document simultaneously in real-time. With co-authoring, users can see each other's changes as they happen, and add comments or track changes as necessary.

Co-authoring is an important tool for teams that need to collaborate on documents, as it streamlines the process and allows for real-time communication and feedback. This feature also enables teams to work more efficiently and complete projects faster, as everyone can contribute and make changes simultaneously.

Document Sharing in Microsoft Word

1. Create a new document or open an existing document that you want to share with others.
2. Click on the "File" tab in the top left corner of the screen, and then click on "Share" in the left-hand menu.
3. Next, select the option that best suits your needs. Here are some examples:
4. Share a Copy: This option allows you to send a copy of the document to others via email, OneDrive, or another cloud storage platform.
5. Invite People: This option enables you to invite people to edit the document, collaborate in real-time, and track changes.

6. Copy Link: This option creates a shareable link to the document, which can be sent via email or instant message.
7. If you select "Invite People," enter the email addresses of the individuals you want to share the document with. You can also add a message to explain why you're sharing the document and set permissions for each user.
8. Once you've set your sharing preferences, click "Share" to send the document to your collaborators.
9. If you've chosen to share via OneDrive or another cloud storage platform, copy the link provided and send it to your collaborators via email or instant message.
10. Collaborators can now open the shared document, edit it, and add comments or track changes as necessary.
11. If you want to see who has access to the shared document or revoke someone's access, click on the "Share" button again and select "Manage Access."

Co-authoring in Microsoft word

1. Create a new document or open an existing document that you want to collaborate on with others.
2. Save the document to a shared location, such as OneDrive or SharePoint, where all collaborators can access it.
3. Click on the "Share" button in the top right corner of the screen.
4. Under "Share with People," enter the email addresses of the individuals you want to collaborate with. You can also add a message to explain why you're sharing the document and set permissions for each user.
5. Once you've set your sharing preferences, click "Share" to send the document to your collaborators.
6. Collaborators can now open the shared document and click the "Edit" button to begin collaborating.

7.   As collaborators make changes to the document, their names will appear in real-time on the upper right corner of the screen.
8.   Collaborators can add comments and track changes as necessary.
9.   To save changes, click on the "Save" button in the top left corner of the screen. This will save the changes made by all collaborators.
10. If someone else is currently editing the document, you will see a message indicating that the document is being edited. You can still view the document but cannot make any changes until the other person is done editing.
11. Once everyone is finished collaborating, click on the "Share" button again and select "Stop Sharing" to revoke access to the document.

Comments

Comments is a way of allowing users to leave notes, questions, or feedback within a document. Comments are useful when collaborating with others on a document, as they provide a way to communicate and discuss specific sections of the document without actually changing the text.

Adding comment to a document in Microsoft word

1.   Select the text you want to comment on.
2.   Go to the "Review" tab at the top of the screen.
3.   Click on the "New Comment" button in the "Comments" section of the ribbon. This will open a comment box in the right margin of the document.
4.   Type your comment in the comment box. You can include as much detail as you need to explain your feedback or ask a question.
5.   If you want to reply to an existing comment, click on the comment box to select it, and then click on the "Reply" button in the "Comments" section of the ribbon.

6. Type your reply in the comment box that appears. Your reply will be indented beneath the original comment.
7. You can also delete comments by selecting the comment box and clicking on the "Delete" button in the "Comments" section of the ribbon.
8. If you want to view or navigate through all the comments in the document, click on the "Comments" button in the "Review" tab.
9. To hide or show all comments in the document, click on the "Show Markup" button in the "Tracking" section of the ribbon and uncheck or check the "Comments" box.

Tracking Changes in Collaboration

Track Changes allows users to keep track of changes made to a document, including edits, deletions, and additions. When this feature is enabled, any changes made to the document are highlighted in a different color than the original text, making them easy to spot.

The tracked changes feature also provides a way for users to add comments and suggestions to the document

Importance of Track Changes

Clarity and transparency: The tracked changes feature makes it easy to see what changes have been made to the document and who made them. This can help to improve clarity and transparency when collaborating with others on a document.

Revision control: The tracked changes feature enables users to keep track of revisions to a document, including who made the changes and when. This can be useful when multiple people are working on the same document, or when making revisions to a document over time.

Feedback and collaboration: By allowing users to add comments and suggestions to the document, the tracked changes feature enables collaboration and feedback between multiple users. This can help to improve the quality of the document and ensure that everyone's input is taken into account.

Efficiency: The tracked changes feature can help to save time when making revisions to a document. Rather than having to manually track changes, users can simply enable this feature and let Word do the work for them.

Accuracy: By highlighting changes in a different color than the original text, the tracked changes feature makes it easy to spot errors or inconsistencies in the document. This can help to improve the accuracy and quality of the final product.

Enabling Track Changes in Microsoft Word

1. Open a document you are collaborating on.
2. Go to the "Review" tab on the ribbon at the top of the screen.
3. Click on the "Track Changes" button in the "Tracking" section of the ribbon. This will enable the track changes feature.
4. Make changes to the document as you normally would. Any changes you make will be highlighted and displayed in a different color than the original text.
5. To accept or reject a change, click on the changed text to select it and then click on the "Accept" or "Reject" button in the "Changes" section of the ribbon.
6. To view a list of all changes made to the document, click on the "Reviewing Pane" button in the "Tracking" section of the ribbon. This will open a pane on the left side of the screen that lists all the changes in chronological order.
7. To hide or show all tracked changes in the document, click on the "Show Markup" button in the "Tracking" section of the ribbon and uncheck or check the boxes for the types of changes you want to see.

8.	To turn off the track changes feature, click on the "Track Changes" button in the "Tracking" section of the ribbon. This will disable the feature and remove all highlighting.

Document Comparison in Microsoft Word

The document comparison feature is a tool that allows users to compare two different versions of a document and highlight any differences between them.

How to compare documents in Microsoft word

1.	Open the two versions of the document that you want to compare.
2.	Click on the "Review" tab in the ribbon.
3.	Click on the "Compare" button in the "Compare" section of the ribbon.
4.	In the "Compare Documents" dialog box, select the original document and the revised document using the "Original document" and "Revised document" drop-down menus.
5.	Choose whether to compare based on specific document elements, such as headers, footers, and tables.
6.	Click on the "OK" button to begin the comparison process.

Once the comparison process is complete, Word will display a new document that highlights all of the differences between the original and revised documents. The differences will be color-coded to indicate whether they were added, deleted, or moved within the document.

Document Protection in Microsoft Word

Document protection is an important way to prevent unauthorized changes, ensure data privacy and maintain document integrity. There are several ways to protect documents in Word, including using password protection, document encryption, and restricted editing.

Password Protection

How to protect your Microsoft word document using password

1. Open the document you want to protect in Microsoft Word.
2. Click on the "File" tab in the ribbon and select "Info".
3. Click on the "Protect Document" button and select "Encrypt with Password".
4. Enter a password in the "Encrypt Document" dialog box and click on "OK".
5. Confirm the password by entering it again and click on "OK".
6. Save the document to apply the password protection.

Restrict Editing Protection

Another way to protect a document in Word is to use the "Restrict Editing" feature. This allows you to control who can make changes to the document, and what kind of changes they can make.

How to restrict editing in a word document

1. Open the document you want to protect in Microsoft Word.
2. Click on the "Review" tab in the ribbon and select "Restrict Editing".
3. In the "Restrict Editing" pane, select the options for what kind of editing is allowed, such as "Tracked changes", "Comments", or "Filling in forms".
4. Click on "Yes, Start Enforcing Protection".
5. Enter a password if desired.
6. Save the document to apply the editing restrictions.

Now, anyone who tries to make changes to the document will be limited to the editing options you selected, and will need to enter a password if one was specified.

Other Microsoft Word Features

Up until this point in the book we have talked about Microsoft features in categories of where they apply. But there are many more hidden Microsoft word features which will drastically help improve your work life

Autocorrect Customization

Autocorrect customization provides several benefits to users. By adding their own custom entries, users can save time and reduce errors by having common spelling and grammar mistakes automatically corrected as they type. This can be particularly useful for words that are frequently mistyped or misspelled. Additionally, users can customize Autocorrect to reflect their own writing style or industry-specific terminology, improving accuracy and efficiency. Customizing Autocorrect can also help users to avoid embarrassing mistakes or typos in professional or personal documents.

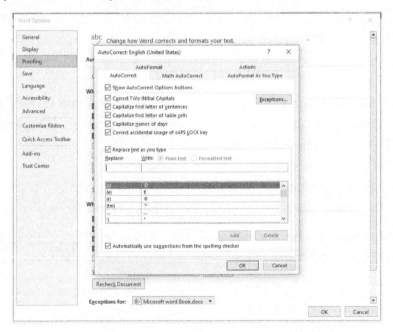

Autocorrect Customization in Microsoft Word

1. Open Microsoft Word and click on the "File" tab in the top left corner of the screen.
2. Click on "Options" at the bottom of the left-hand menu.
3. In the Word Options window, select "Proofing" from the left-hand menu.
4. Click on the "Autocorrect Options" button at the top of the window.
5. In the Autocorrect window, you can add your own custom entries or modify existing ones. For example, you can add a common misspelling and set it to be automatically corrected to the correct spelling.
6. To add a new autocorrect entry, click on the "Add" button in the Autocorrect window.
7. In the "Replace" box, type the misspelled word or phrase that you want to correct.
8. In the "With" box, type the correct spelling or phrase that you want to replace the misspelled word or phrase with.
9. Click on the "OK" button to save the new Autocorrect entry.
10. To modify an existing Autocorrect entry, select the entry from the list in the Autocorrect window and click on the "Modify" button.
11. Make the necessary changes to the "Replace" and "With" boxes, and click on the "OK" button to save the changes.
12. You can also delete an Autocorrect entry by selecting it from the list and clicking on the "Delete" button.
13. Once you have made all of the desired changes to the Autocorrect feature, click on the "OK" button in the Autocorrect window and then click on the "OK" button in the Word Options window to close it.

Custom Ribbon and toolbar

Custom Ribbon and Toolbar is a feature that was introduced in Microsoft office 2007 to allow users to create their own customized interface for frequently used commands and tools. With Custom Ribbon, users can create a new tab on the Ribbon and add their preferred commands and tools to it. This allows them to easily access their most commonly used features in one convenient location thereby reducing the time wasted searching for specific tools. Similarly, with Custom Toolbar, users can create a new toolbar and add frequently used commands to it. This can be particularly useful for users who have specialized workflows or need quick access to specific tools.

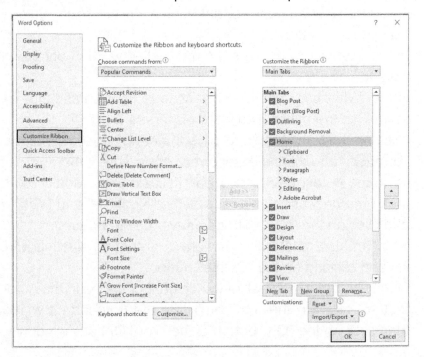

Step to creating a custom Ribbon and Toolbar

Custom Ribbon

1.   Open Microsoft Word and click on "File" in the top left corner of the screen.

2.   Click on "Options" and select "Customize Ribbon" in the left-hand menu.
3.   Click on "New Tab" to create a new tab in the Ribbon.
4.   Rename the new tab by clicking on the "New Tab (Custom)" and typing a new name.
5.   Add commands to the new tab by clicking on the "New Group" button.
6.   Rename the new group by clicking on the "New Group (Custom)" and typing a new name.
7.   Select the commands you want to add from the left-hand menu and click the "Add" button.
8.   Rearrange the order of the commands by using the up and down arrows.
9.   Click "OK" to save your changes.

Custom Toolbar

1.   Right-click on the Ribbon and select "Customize the Ribbon."
2.   Click on "New Tab" and rename the tab.
3.   Click on "New Group" and rename the group.
4.   Click on "Commands Not in the Ribbon" in the left-hand menu.
5.   Select the command you want to add and drag it to the new group on the Custom Toolbar.
6.   Rearrange the order of the commands by dragging them up or down.
7.   Click "OK" to save your changes.

Language Customization

Language customization allows users to adjust various settings related to the language of their document.

Adjusting Language in Microsoft Word

1. Open Microsoft Word and click on the "Review" tab in the Ribbon.
2. Click on the "Language" button in the "Proofing" group.
3. From the drop-down menu, select "Set Proofing Language."
4. In the "Language" dialog box, choose the language you want to use for proofing, such as English (United States).
5. Check the box next to "Detect language automatically" if you want Word to automatically identify the language of your document.
6. Check the box next to "Do not check spelling or grammar" if you want to exclude specific text from the spelling and grammar check.
7. Click "OK" to save your changes.

Custom Dictionaries

Sometimes you want to add specialized terminology or proper names to the spelling and grammar check, or you want to exclude certain words or phrases from being marked as errors. This can be done using custom dictionaries. Custom dictionaries are user-created dictionaries that allow you to add new words or phrases to the spelling and grammar check.

Creating and adding words to custom dictionaries

1. Open Microsoft Word and click on the "File" tab.
2. Select "Options" from the menu.
3. Click on "Proofing" in the left-hand menu.
4. Click on "Custom Dictionaries."
5. Click on "New" to create a new custom dictionary.
6. Enter a name for the dictionary and click "Save."
7. To add words to the custom dictionary, click "Edit Word List" and type in the words you want to add.
8. Click "Add" after each word to add it to the dictionary.
9. Click "OK" to save the custom dictionary.
10. To use the custom dictionary, select "Custom Dictionaries" from the "Proofing" section of the "Options" dialog box.

11. Select the custom dictionary you want to use and click "Change Default."

12. Click "OK" to save your changes.

Automation and Advanced Customization

Automation refers to the use of tools and features to automate repetitive or time-consuming tasks, making it easier and more efficient to work with large or complex documents. There are several ways to automate tasks in Word, including macros, templates, and add-ins. Automation helps to improve overall productivity of a user by handling re-occurrent tasks while providing the user more time to focus on other important tasks or activities that require their attention and creativity. By automating repetitive or time-consuming tasks, users can work more efficiently and effectively, reducing errors and increasing productivity. This can be particularly helpful when working with large or complex documents, where automation can help streamline workflows and ensure consistency across multiple documents.

Macros

A macro is a series of recorded actions that can be played back to automate repetitive tasks. In Word, macros can be created using the Macro Recorder or by writing Visual Basic for Applications (VBA) code. Some common examples of tasks that can be automated with macros include formatting, inserting text or graphics, and performing calculations.

Creating Macros Using Visual Basic Application (Code Style)

1. Create a new document or open an existing one.
2. Click on the "View" tab on the ribbon at the top of the screen.
3. You can also find it on the "Developers Tab" (Hidden by default)
4. In the "Macros" section, click on "Macros" to open the Macros dialog box.
5. In the Macros dialog box, enter a name for your new macro in the "Macro name" field.

6. Click on the "Create" button to open the Visual Basic Editor.
7. In the Visual Basic Editor, enter the code for your macro. For example, if you want to create a macro that inserts a specific block of text, you might enter code like this:
8. Sub InsertText() Selection.TypeText Text:="The text you want to insert." End Sub
9. Save your macro by clicking on the "Save" button in the Visual Basic Editor.
10. Close the Visual Basic Editor and return to your Word document.
11. To run your macro, go back to the "View" tab and click on "Macros" again.
12. In the Macros dialog box, select your macro from the list and click on the "Run" button to execute it.
13. Your macro will perform the actions you specified in the code, such as inserting text or formatting your document.

Creating Macro Using Microsoft Word Macro recorder (No Code)

1. Create a new document or open an existing one.
2. Click on the "View" tab on the ribbon at the top of the screen.
3. In the "Macros" section, click on "Record Macro" to open the Record Macro dialog box.
4. In the Record Macro dialog box, enter a name for your new macro in the "Macro name" field.
5. Choose a location to store the macro (either in the current document or in your global template).
6. Optionally, assign a keyboard shortcut or button to your macro.
7. Click "OK" to start recording your macro.
8. Perform the actions you want to automate in your Word document (such as formatting text, inserting images, or running a spell check).
9. Once you've completed the actions, click on "Stop Recording" in the "Macros" section of the ribbon.

Running a Saved Macro

1. Create a new document or open an existing one.
2. Click on the "View" tab on the ribbon at the top of the screen.
3. In the "Macros" section, click on "Macros" to open the Macros dialog box.
4. In the Macros dialog box, you will see a list of available macros.
5. Select the macro you want to run from the list.
6. Click on the "Run" button to execute the selected macro.

The selected macro will now perform the actions it was programmed to do. The specific actions can vary depending on the macro you created or saved.

If you assigned a keyboard shortcut or toolbar button to the macro during its creation, you can also use that shortcut or button to run the macro without going through the Macros dialog box.

Templates

A template is a pre-designed document that can be customized and used as a starting point for new documents. Templates can be used to automate the creation of documents with a consistent layout, style, and formatting. Word includes several built-in templates, and you can also create your own templates.

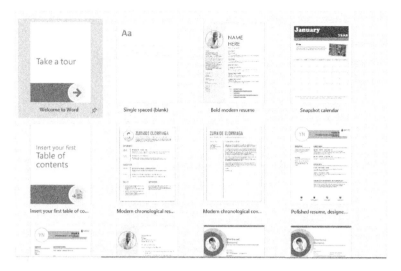

Creating a Template in Microsoft Word

1. Open the document you wish to use as a template.
2. Customize the document with the desired formatting, styles, and content that you want to include in your template.
3. Once your document is formatted and designed the way you want, click on the "File" tab in the ribbon at the top of the screen.
4. Select "Save As" from the options.
5. In the Save As dialog box, choose the location where you want to save the template.
6. Enter a name for your template in the "File name" field.
7. Select "Word Template (.*dotx*)" or "*Word Macro-Enabled Template* (.dotm)" from the "Save as type" dropdown menu, depending on whether you want to include macros in your template or not.
8. Click on the "Save" button to save the template.

Selecting and Using your Custom Template

1. Open Microsoft Word.
2. Click on the "File" tab and select "New".
3. In the New Document window, click on "Custom" in the left pane.

4. Select the template you created from the list of available templates.
5. Click on the "Create" button to create a new document based on the template.

Add-ins

An add-in is a program that extends the functionality of Word by adding new features or tools. Add-ins can be used to automate tasks that are not possible with Word's built-in tools, such as data analysis or translation. Word includes several built-in add-ins, and you can also download and install add-ins from the Microsoft Office Store.

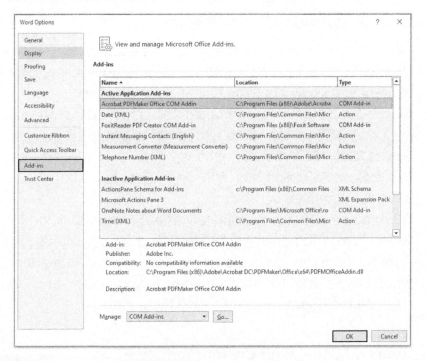

Installing Custom Add-ins in Microsoft Word

1. Open Microsoft Word.
2. Click on the "File" tab in the ribbon at the top of the screen.
3. Select "Options" from the menu on the left side of the screen.

4. In the Word Options window, select "Add-Ins" from the menu on the left.
5. At the bottom of the screen, you will see a dropdown menu labeled "Manage." Select "COM Add-ins" from the list.
6. Click on the "Go" button next to the dropdown menu.
7. In the COM Add-Ins window, click on the "Add" button.
8. Navigate to the location where the add-in file is saved on your computer.
9. Select the add-in file and click on the "Open" button.
10. The add-in will now be added to the list of available add-ins in the COM Add-Ins window.
11. Check the box next to the add-in you want to enable.
12. Click on the "OK" button to close the COM Add-Ins window.
13. Restart Microsoft Word for the changes to take effect.

Quick Parts

Quick Parts is a feature that allows a user to save and reuse snippets of text or graphics. It allows you to create reusable content that you can quickly insert into your documents, such as headers and footers, watermarks, page numbers, and frequently used paragraphs or phrases.

Quick parts are very useful in automation as it allows a user to save time and effort by adding elements in one click.

Creating a Quick Part

1. Select the text or graphic you want to save as a Quick Part.
2. Go to the "Insert" tab on the ribbon.
3. Click on "Quick Parts" in the "Text" group.
4. Select "Save Selection to Quick Part Gallery" from the dropdown menu.
5. In the "Create New Building Block" window, enter a name for the Quick Part in the "Name" field.

6.   Select a category for the Quick Part from the "Category" dropdown menu.
7.   Enter a description of the Quick Part in the "Description" field (optional).
8.   Click on the "OK" button to save the Quick Part.

Reusing a Quick part

1.   Create a new document.
2.   Place the cursor where you want to insert the Quick Part.
3.   Go to the "Insert" tab on the ribbon.
4.   Click on "Quick Parts" in the "Text" group.
5.   Select the Quick Part you want to insert from the dropdown menu.
6.   The Quick Part will be inserted into your document at the cursor location.

Building Blocks

Building Blocks are pre-designed content elements, such as text, graphics, or tables, that can be easily inserted into a document. They are similar to Quick Parts, but typically contain more complex formatting and may include multiple elements.

Some popular examples of Building Blocks:

Cover Pages: Professionally designed cover pages that can be easily customized with your own text and graphics.

Headers and Footers: Pre-designed headers and footers that can be easily inserted into a document and customized as needed.

Tables: Pre-designed tables with custom formatting that can be inserted into a document and customized as needed.

Page Borders: Pre-designed page borders that can be easily inserted into a document to add visual interest.

Creating a Building Block

1. Select the content you want to save as a Building Block. This can include text, graphics, tables, or any other content element you want to reuse in future documents.
2. Format the content as desired, including font styles, colors, borders, and other formatting options.
3. Select the content again, and then go to the "Insert" tab on the ribbon.
4. Click on "Quick Parts" in the "Text" group, and then select "Save Selection to Quick Part Gallery" from the dropdown menu.
5. In the "Create New Building Block" dialog box that appears, enter a name for the Building Block in the "Name" field. This should be a descriptive name that will help you easily identify the Building Block in the future.
6. Choose a category for the Building Block from the "Category" dropdown menu. You can select an existing category or create a new one by clicking on "Create New Category."
7. Enter a description for the Building Block in the "Description" field. This is optional, but can be helpful for providing additional context about the Building Block.
8. Use the "Gallery" options to specify where you want the Building Block to appear in the Quick Parts gallery. You can choose to display the Building Block in the "General" gallery or in a specific category.
9. Click "OK" to save the Building Block to the gallery.

Once you have saved a Building Block to the gallery, you can easily insert it into future documents by going to the "Insert" tab, clicking on "Quick Parts," and selecting the appropriate Building Block from the gallery. You can also edit or delete Building Blocks by right-clicking on them in the gallery and selecting the appropriate option.

Field Codes

Field codes are used to insert dynamic content in a document. These are special placeholders that reference a value, such as a date, time, page number, or document properties.

Using field codes in Microsoft Word can be a powerful way to add dynamic content to your documents, such as automatically updating dates or page numbers.

Using Field codes to add dynamic content to a document

1. Position the cursor where you want to insert the field code.
2. Press "Ctrl + F9" to insert the field code brackets. Alternatively, you can go to the "Insert" tab, click "Quick Parts" in the "Text" group, and select "Field" from the dropdown menu.
3. Within the field code brackets, type the name of the field code you want to insert. For example, to insert the current date, type "DATE" within the brackets.
4. Press "F9" to update the field code and display the current value. Alternatively, you can right-click on the field code and select "Update Field" from the context menu.
5. To customize a field code, right-click on it and select "Edit Field" from the context menu. In the "Field Options" dialog box, you can choose different formats, switches, and properties for the field.
6. To view all the field codes in a document, press "Alt + F9". This will toggle between displaying the field codes and displaying the results of the field codes.
7. To lock a field code so that it doesn't update automatically, select the field code and press "Ctrl + F11". To unlock a field code, select it and press "Ctrl + Shift + F11".

Productivity in Microsoft word

With everything you have learned so far, you should be able to use Microsoft Word like a pro. With the help of automation tools such as macros, templates, and add-ins, your work style in Microsoft Word should have improved significantly, allowing you to save time and effort.

Now we are going to be talking about some important tips to improving your productivity in Microsoft word using the tools we have discussed so far.

Tips to increasing productivity in Microsoft Word

Use templates: Templates can save time by providing a pre-formatted document with the correct layout and styles. You can create your own templates or use the pre-installed templates in Microsoft Word.

Use keyboard shortcuts: Keyboard shortcuts are an efficient way to save time while working in Microsoft Word. A study conducted by Microsoft found that users who used keyboard shortcuts to perform tasks in Word were up to 10 times faster than those who used menus. keyboard shortcuts can be particularly effective for frequently used tasks, such as copying and pasting, formatting text, and saving documents. At the end of this book, I have included up to 90 Microsoft word keyboard shortcuts.

Use styles: Styles can help you quickly format your document with consistent headings, font sizes, and spacing. By using styles and custom styles, you can apply changes to the entire document with just a few clicks and save yourself a tremendous amount of time especially when you are working with multiple documents following the same formatting.

Use AutoCorrect: AutoCorrect can save time by automatically correcting common spelling errors and typos as you type. You can also create your own AutoCorrect entries for frequently used phrases.

Use Find and Replace: Find and Replace is a powerful tool that can save time by quickly replacing all occurrences of a word or phrase in a document.

Use Quick Parts: Quick Parts are pre-defined blocks of text that can be inserted into a document with just a few clicks. You can create your own Quick Parts for frequently used text, such as your company address or signature.

Use Macros: Macros are a way to automate repetitive tasks in Microsoft Word. You can create your own macros or use pre-built macros to automate tasks such as formatting, inserting text, and generating reports.

There are numerous ways to enhance productivity in Microsoft Word, and the more frequently you use the application, the more you'll discover its immense value in your daily work life.

Extra Resources

Microsoft Word Shortcuts

A comprehensive compilation of Microsoft Word shortcuts, meticulously gathered to assist you in maximizing productivity. With these time-saving keystrokes at your fingertips, you'll navigate Word with finesse, accomplishing tasks more efficiently than ever before. Whether you're a seasoned Word user or just starting your journey, this exhaustive list of shortcuts will empower you to streamline your workflow, reduce repetitive actions, and unleash the full potential of this powerful word processing tool.

Navigation:

Ctrl + Left Arrow: Move cursor one word to the left

Ctrl + Right Arrow: Move cursor one word to the right

Ctrl + Up Arrow: Move cursor to the beginning of the previous paragraph

Ctrl + Down Arrow: Move cursor to the beginning of the next paragraph

Ctrl + Home: Move to the beginning of the document

Ctrl + End: Move to the end of the document

Ctrl + Page Up: Move to the previous page

Ctrl + Page Down: Move to the next page

Ctrl + Arrow keys: Move one word or one paragraph at a time

Alt + Ctrl + Page Up: Switch to the previous window

Alt + Ctrl + Page Down: Switch to the next window

Ctrl + G: Go to a page, bookmark, footnote, table, comment, graphic, or other location

Ctrl + F6: Switch to the next document window

Ctrl + Shift + F6: Switch to the previous document window

F6: Move to the next pane or frame

Shift + F6: Move to the previous pane or frame

Selection:

Shift + Arrow keys: Select text

Shift + Home: Select from the insertion point to the beginning of the line

Shift + End: Select from the insertion point to the end of the line

Ctrl + Shift + Home: Select from the insertion point to the beginning of the document

Ctrl + Shift + End: Select from the insertion point to the end of the document

F8: Turn on extend mode

Shift + Left Arrow: Select one character to the left

Shift + Right Arrow: Select one character to the right

Shift + Ctrl + Left Arrow: Select one word to the left

Shift + Ctrl + Right Arrow: Select one word to the right

Shift + Ctrl + Up Arrow: Select from the cursor to the beginning of the current paragraph

Shift + Ctrl + Down Arrow: Select from the cursor to the beginning of the next paragraph

Ctrl + A: Select all

Ctrl + Shift + F8: Turn on extend selection mode

Esc: Cancel a selection

Editing:

Ctrl + C: Copy selected text or object

Ctrl + X: Cut selected text or object

Ctrl + V: Paste copied or cut text or object

Ctrl + Z: Undo the last action

Ctrl + Y: Redo the last action

Ctrl + F: Find text in the document

Ctrl + H: Find and replace text in the document

Ctrl + D: Open the font dialog box

Ctrl + E: Center selected text or object

Ctrl + L: Left align selected text or object

Ctrl + R: Right align selected text or object

Ctrl + J: Justify selected text or object

Ctrl + K: Insert a hyperlink

Ctrl + N: Create a new document

Ctrl + O: Open an existing document

Ctrl + S: Save the current document

Ctrl + W: Close the current document

Ctrl + P: Print the current document

F3: Insert an AutoText entry or quickly find and replace text

Shift + F3: Change the case of letters

Formatting:

Ctrl + I: Italicize selected text

Ctrl + U: Underline selected text

Ctrl + Shift + A: Change selected text to all caps

Ctrl + Shift + L: Apply bullets or numbering to selected text

Ctrl + Shift + C: Copy formatting from selected text

Ctrl + Shift + V: Paste formatting to selected text

Ctrl + Shift + D: Double underline selected text

Ctrl + Shift + E: Track changes

Ctrl + B: Apply bold formatting to selected text

Ctrl + D: Open the Font dialog box

Ctrl + E: Center selected text or align it to the right or left margin

Ctrl + J: Justify selected text or align it to both margins

Ctrl + L: Align selected text to the left margin

Ctrl + R: Align selected text to the right margin

Ctrl + Q: Remove paragraph formatting

Ctrl + T: Create a hanging indent

Ctrl + Shift + >: Increase font size by one point

Ctrl + Shift + <: Decrease font size by one point

Ctrl + Shift + H: Apply hidden text formatting

Ctrl + Shift + W: Underline selected words, but not spaces

Ctrl + Shift + S: Apply a style

Ctrl + Shift + F: Change the font of selected text

Ctrl + Shift + K: Format selected text as small caps

Ctrl + Shift + N: Apply normal style to selected text

Ctrl + Shift + P: Change the font size of selected text

Ctrl + Shift + Q: Remove paragraph formatting from selected text

Ctrl + Shift + T: Create a hanging indent

Ctrl + Shift + W: Underline selected words, but not spaces

Review:

F7: Check spelling and grammar

Shift + F7: Open the thesaurus

Alt + Ctrl + M: Insert a comment

Ctrl + Shift + E: Turn Track Changes on or off

Ctrl + Shift + G: Open the Word count dialog box

Ctrl + Shift + H: Apply hidden text formatting to selected text

Ctrl + Shift + S: Open the Style pane

Ctrl + Shift + X: Mark selected text as excluded from proofing

Ctrl + Shift + Z: Switch between the last four cursor positions

Alt + Shift + R: Insert a trademark symbol

Alt + Shift + C: Insert a copyright symbol

Alt + Shift + P: Insert a section symbol

Microsoft Add-Ins

Below I have compiled a list of useful Microsoft word add-ins which will add more extra features to your Microsoft Word application or to help improve your productivity when using Microsoft word.

1. **Grammarly:** Grammarly is an essential add-in for writers. It helps improve your writing by providing real-time grammar and spelling suggestions. It highlights errors and offers suggestions to enhance the clarity and correctness of your text.

2. **Translator:** The Translator add-in enables quick and convenient translation of text within Word documents. It supports various languages, allowing you to easily translate words, phrases, or entire paragraphs without leaving the Word interface.

3. **DocuSign:** DocuSign revolutionizes the process of signing and managing documents. With this add-in, you can electronically sign and send documents for signature directly within Word, eliminating the need for printing, scanning, or mailing physical copies.

4. **Wikipedia:** The Wikipedia add-in brings the vast knowledge of Wikipedia right into Word. It allows you to search for and access Wikipedia articles without having to switch between applications, making it convenient for quick reference and research.

5. **Evernote:** Evernote integration allows you to seamlessly connect Word with your Evernote account. It enables you to capture and save ideas, research, and notes directly from Word, making it easy to organize and access your content across devices.

6. **Thesaurus:** The Thesaurus add-in is a valuable tool for improving your vocabulary. It provides a built-in thesaurus, allowing you to find synonyms and antonyms for words, enhancing your writing by offering alternative word choices.

7. **MindManager:** MindManager is a powerful add-in for brainstorming and visual thinking. It lets you create mind maps,

flowcharts, and diagrams directly within Word, helping you organize ideas and improve your thought process.

8. **Read Mode:** Read Mode is a feature that optimizes the document layout for a distraction-free reading experience. It hides menus and toolbars, allowing you to focus solely on reading the content without any distractions.

9. **SmartDraw:** SmartDraw is a versatile diagramming tool that seamlessly integrates with Word. It provides a wide range of templates and tools to create professional diagrams, flowcharts, organizational charts, and more, enhancing the visual appeal and clarity of your documents.

10. **Dropbox:** The Dropbox add-in simplifies file management and collaboration. It allows you to access and share your Dropbox files directly from Word, making it easy to collaborate with others, sync documents across devices, and ensure the latest versions are always available.

11. **Adobe Sign:** Adobe Sign is a popular e-signature solution that streamlines the signing process. With the Adobe Sign add-in, you can securely sign and send documents for electronic signature within Word, eliminating the need for physical signatures and paperwork.

12. **EndNote:** EndNote is a powerful reference management tool for academic and research writing. It allows you to insert and format citations and bibliographies in Word, making it effortless to manage your sources and create accurate and consistent references.

13. **LinkedIn Resume Assistant:** The LinkedIn Resume Assistant add-in provides valuable assistance in creating professional resumes. It offers personalized suggestions, examples, and tips based on millions of LinkedIn profiles, helping you craft an impressive and tailored resume.

14. **Adobe Stock**: Adobe Stock integrates a vast library of high-quality images, illustrations, and graphics directly within Word. It allows you to browse, preview, and license images without leaving the application, making it convenient for enhancing the visual appeal of your documents.

15. **OfficeMaps:** OfficeMaps is a useful add-in for creating and visualizing floor plans and office layouts. It provides tools to design and customize floor plans, helping you communicate spatial information effectively within Word documents.

16. **Wikipedia Images:** This add-in allows you to search for and insert Wikipedia images directly into Word. It saves you time and effort by eliminating the need to search for images separately and then insert them into your documents.

17. **Code Format:** Code Format is a handy add-in for developers and programmers. It formats code snippets with syntax highlighting, making them more readable and preserving the formatting when pasted into Word from programming environments.

18. **GIPHY:** GIPHY brings the world of animated GIFs into Word. With this add-in, you can search and insert GIFs from the extensive GIPHY library, adding fun and visual appeal to your documents and presentations.

19. **OfficeMaps Planner:** OfficeMaps Planner helps you manage and visualize tasks and projects within Word. It provides a simple and intuitive interface to create and track project plans, assign tasks, and monitor progress, seamlessly integrating project management into your documents.

20. **EasyBib:** EasyBib is another popular citation generator for academic writing. This add-in automates the process of creating citations and bibliographies in various citation styles, such as APA, MLA, and Chicago, saving you time and ensuring accurate referencing.

21. **Office QR:** Office QR enables you to generate QR codes for specific actions within Word. These QR codes can include actions like calling a phone number, sending an email, or opening a website, providing an interactive and convenient experience for readers of your documents.

22. **Noun Project:** Noun Project offers a vast collection of high-quality icons and symbols. With the Noun Project add-in, you can search and insert icons directly into Word, enhancing visual communication and adding clarity to your documents.

23. **Symbols & Characters:** Symbols & Characters add-in provides quick access to a wide range of symbols, special characters, and emoji within Word. It simplifies the process of inserting special characters, mathematical symbols, currency signs, and other symbols into your documents.

24. **Merriam-Webster Dictionary:** Merriam-Webster Dictionary add-in brings a comprehensive dictionary and thesaurus directly into Word. It provides definitions, synonyms, antonyms, and pronunciation guides, allowing you to enhance your writing and improve language accuracy.

25. **Bibliography Helper:** Bibliography Helper simplifies the process of creating bibliographies and reference lists. It offers templates and tools to manage sources, format citations, and generate accurate bibliographies within Word, ensuring consistency and adherence to citation styles.

26. **ProWritingAid:** ProWritingAid is a comprehensive writing assistant that offers advanced grammar, style, and readability analysis. This add-in helps you improve your writing by providing in-depth insights and suggestions to enhance clarity, tone, and overall writing quality.

27. **Track Changes:** Track Changes is a built-in feature in Word that allows collaborators to review, edit, and leave comments on

documents. This feature enables multiple users to work on the same document while tracking and managing revisions, ensuring transparency and effective collaboration.

28. **OneDrive:** OneDrive is Microsoft's cloud storage and file synchronization service. The OneDrive add-in simplifies the process of accessing and sharing your OneDrive files directly within Word, providing seamless integration for efficient collaboration and document management.

29. **Onetastic:** Onetastic is a popular add-in for Microsoft Word that enhances its functionality and provides additional features and tools. It is designed to improve productivity and streamline various tasks within Word.

30. **TextExpander:** TextExpander is a powerful add-in for Microsoft Word that helps users increase productivity and save time by automating the typing of frequently used text snippets or phrases.

31. **Translate:** The Translate add-in provides instant translation of selected text or entire documents within Word. It supports a wide range of languages, making it useful for international communication and understanding.

32. **Focus Writer:** Focus Writer is an add-in that helps you concentrate on your writing by providing a distraction-free writing environment. It eliminates distractions, such as menus and toolbars, allowing you to focus solely on your content.

33. **Kutools:** Kutools for Word is a powerful add-in that extends the functionality of Microsoft Word and provides a wide range of tools and features to enhance productivity

What Next?

Congratulations for reaching this point in your journey to becoming a Microsoft word expert. Up until this point you have gone through a lot of features of Microsoft word, but that's not all, there are lot more features and things you can achieve with Microsoft word and here I have compiled a list of ten websites where you can learn more about Microsoft Word, collaborate with Microsoft word experts, learn about new updates and features and many more adventure waiting for you. I wish you and best and Goodluck.

1. Microsoft Office Support (support.microsoft.com)
2. Microsoft Office Templates (templates.office.com)
3. GCF LearnFree (edu.gcfglobal.org)
4. WordTips (word.tips.net)
5. TechBoomers (techboomers.com)
6. TutorialsPoint (tutorialspoint.com)
7. Word MVP Site (word.mvps.org)
8. WordGuru (wordguru.com)
9. FreeTrainingTutorials (freetrainingtutorials.com)
10. WordEasy (wordeasy.com)

EXERCISES

A compilation of 36 exercise questions awaits you, designed to challenge your knowledge, skills, and expertise in Microsoft Word. These exercises have been carefully curated to cover various aspects of Word, ranging from basic functionalities to advanced techniques. Whether you are a beginner looking to solidify your foundation or an experienced user seeking to push the boundaries of your expertise, these exercises will put your Microsoft Word proficiency to the test.

In this comprehensive collection, you will find exercises that encompass different areas of Word usage. From document creation and formatting to advanced features such as macros, collaboration, and document protection, each exercise is meticulously crafted to assess your understanding and command over the application.

The exercises are designed to mimic real-life scenarios and tasks commonly encountered in professional settings. You will be challenged to perform tasks such as creating and formatting tables, generating complex page layouts, utilizing advanced formatting features, working with images and shapes, and mastering the art of efficient document management.

Beginner Level Exercise

1.   Create a new blank document and save it with a custom name.

2.   Format a selected paragraph with bold and italic styles.

3.   Insert a bulleted list and apply a specific bullet style.

4.   Change the font size of a selected text to a specific value.

5.   Align a paragraph to the center of the page.

6.   Insert a page break to start a new page.

7.   Apply a specific page border to a document.

8.   Insert a picture from a file and remove the background.

9.   Create a simple table with three columns and three rows.

Intermediate Level Exercise

10.   Apply different heading styles to sections of a document.

11.   Insert and format a SmartArt graphic.

12.   Use the "Find and Replace" feature to replace specific words throughout a document.

13.   Create and modify a multi-level numbered list.

14.   Use the spelling and grammar checker to correct errors in a document

15.   Format selected text as a hyperlink.

16.   Insert and format a text box with specific borders and fill color.

17.   Use the Track Changes feature to review and accept/reject changes made to a document.

18.   Create a custom table of contents with hyperlinks.

19.   Use the Mail Merge feature to create personalized letters or labels.

Advanced Level Exercise

20.   Create a custom Word template with specific styles and formatting.

21.   Create and apply a custom style set to a document.

22.   Customize the ribbon by adding or removing commands.

23.   Insert and format a cross-reference to a specific section or figure in the document.

24.   Record and run a simple macro to automate a repetitive task.

25. Collaborate on a document with others using real-time co-authoring.

26. Protect a document with a password and specific editing restrictions.

27. Customize the table properties, such as cell alignment, borders, and shading.

Expert Level Exercise

28. Create a custom table style and apply it to a complex table with merged cells.

29. Use advanced features like sorting and filtering to organize data in a table.

30. Customize the building blocks and create your own Quick Parts for easy reuse.

31. Utilize advanced page layout options like multiple columns, sections, and breaks.

32. Create a master document with subdocuments and apply consistent formatting throughout.

33. Utilize the document comparison feature to compare two different versions of a document.

34. Insert and format a complex mathematical equation using the Equation Editor.

35. Create a custom watermark and apply it to specific pages or throughout the document.

36. Utilize the Advanced Find feature to search for and replace specific formatting in a document.

Printed in Great Britain
by Amazon

26001620R00066